POLITICS AND AMERICAN BUSINESS

THE GROWTH OF INDUSTRIAL AMERICA
1860-1960

by Edward F. Mannino

WingSpan Press

Published in the United States and the United Kingdom by WingSpan Press, Livermore, CA

The WingSpan name, logo and colophon are the trademarks of WingSpan Publishing.

ISBN 978-1-59594-590-7 (pbk.)
ISBN 978-1-59594-913-4 (ebk.)

First edition 2016

Printed in the United States of America

www.wingspanpress.com

Library of Congress Control Number: 2016945531

1 2 3 4 5 6 7 8 9 10

FOR MY GRANDSONS,
HENRY AND GEORGE MANNINO

"After all, the chief business of the American people is business....
Wealth is the product of industry, ambition, character and untiring effort"
    —Calvin Coolidge

"The sole function of government is to bring about a condition of affairs favorable to the beneficial development of private enterprise"
    —Herbert Hoover

"There is nobody in this country who got rich on his own. Nobody. You built a factory out there? Good for you. But I wanna be clear. You moved your goods to market on the roads the rest of us paid for. You hired workers the rest of us paid to educate. You were safe in your factory because of police forces and fire forces that the rest of us paid for."
    —Elizabeth Warren

CONTENTS

Chronology ii

Introduction.. 1

Chapter One - The Civil War: Crushing the Slave
        Power 11

Chapter Two - The Ascent of Business: Fueling
        Economic Development..38

Chapter Three - The Advent of Regulation: The
        Producers Strike Back...55

Chapter Four - The Second Round of Regulation:
        The Progressive Movement 81

Chapter Five - From Confrontation to Cooperation:
        World War I, Business, and the Return of
        Republican Rule.. 112

Chapter Six – Regulation With a Vengeance: FDR's
        New Deals... 128

Chapter Seven – The Military-Industrial Complex:
        World War II, The Cold War, and American
        Business 152

Conclusion: The Intersecting Spheres of
        Government and Business.................................... 169

Notes 184

Index 195

About the Author..202

CHRONOLOGY

1860 – Abraham Lincoln, the first Republican
       president, elected

1860-1890 – 440,000 U.S. patents granted

1861-1865 – The American Civil War

1861 – Morrill Protective Tariff Act enacted

1862 – Homestead Act, Pacific Railway Act, and
       Morrill Land Grant Act all enacted

1863 – National Bank Act enacted

1864 – Lincoln reelected

1865 – Lincoln assassinated; Civil War ends; Andrew
       Johnson becomes president

1865-1875 – Buffalo population decreased from 15
       million to 200,000

1865-1890 – 9 to 10 million immigrants legally enter
       United States

1866-1877 – 11 steel mills built in United States using
       Bessemer Process

1867 – Grange (Patrons of Husbandry) founded

1867-1890 – 8 new states added to Union (Nebraska,
       Colorado, North Dakota, South Dakota,
       Montana, Washington, Idaho, and Wyoming)

1868 – Republican Ulysses Grant elected president;
       Knights of Labor founded

1869 – Union Pacific and Central Pacific Railroads
       meet in Utah to complete first transcontinental
       railroad

1870-1890 – U.S. population increases from 6.8

million to 16.7 million; population west of Mississippi River more than doubles

1872 – Grant reelected

1873 – Timber Culture Act enacted

1874 – Barbed wire invented by J.F. Glidden

1876 – Republican Rutherford Hayes elected president

1877 – Desert Land Act enacted; Munn v. Illinois decided, upholding Granger Laws; Great Railroad Strike

1877-1890s – Farmers' Alliances active

1878 – Timber and Stone Act enacted

1880 – Republican James Garfield elected president

1882 – Trust Device invented by Standard Oil

1883 – Four transcontinental railroads in service, including a southern route

1884 – Democrat Grover Cleveland elected president

1886 – Haymarket Square Riot in Chicago

1887 – Interstate Commerce Act enacted

1888 – Republican Benjamin Harrison elected president

1889 – Jane Addams opens first settlement house in Chicago; Progressive Movement begins

1890 – Sherman Antitrust Act enacted

1892 – Cleveland elected president for second time, in a nonconsecutive term; Populist Omaha Platform and Convention; Populists poll 1 million votes and win 22 electoral votes; Homestead Steel Strike in Pennsylvania

1894 – Pullman Company National Strike

1895 – Supreme Court upholds Eugene Debs' conviction for ignoring Pullman Strike injunction; Supreme Court also rules Sugar Trust mergers did not violate Sherman Antitrust Act and strikes down income tax as unconstitutional; National Association of Manufacturers founded

1896 – Republican William McKinley defeats Democrat/Populist William Jennings Bryan for president

1900 – McKinley reelected, again defeating Bryan

1901 – McKinley assassinated and Vice President Theodore Roosevelt becomes president; Frank Norris' The Octopus published; American Medical Association founded

1902 – Anthracite Strike

1903 – Elkins Act enacted; Department of Commerce established

1904 – Roosevelt elected president; Ida Tarbell's History of the Standard Oil Company published; Supreme Court decides Northern Securities Co. v. United States

1906 – Upton Sinclair's The Jungle published; Pure Food and Drug Act enacted; Meat Inspection Law enacted; Hepburn Act enacted; David Graham Phillips' The Treason of the Senate published

1907 – Panic of 1907; Walter Rauschenbusch's Christianity and the Social Crisis published

1908 – Republican William Howard Taft elected president

1909 – Payne-Aldrich Tariff passed; Herbert Hoover's Principles of Mining published

1910 – Mann-Elkins Act enacted; Theodore Roosevelt delivers "New Nationalism" speech

1911 – Supreme Court decides Standard Oil Co. v. United States and establishes the "Rule of Reason" in antitrust litigation

1912 – Democrat Woodrow Wilson defeats Taft and Progressive Party candidate Theodore Roosevelt; U.S. Chamber of Commerce founded

1913 – 16th (income tax) and 17th (direct election of senators) Amendments ratified; Federal Reserve Act enacted and Federal Reserve System established; Underwood-Simmons Tariff passed

1914 – Clayton Antitrust Act enacted; Federal Trade Commission Act enacted

1914-1918 – World War I

1916 – Wilson reelected; Federal Farm Loan Act enacted; Warehouse Act enacted; Revenue Act raises taxes

1917 – United States enters World War I; War Industries Board established; Railroad Administration established; Food Administration established; Fuel Administration established; union membership of approximately 3 million

1919 – 18th Amendment (prohibition) ratified

1920 – Republican Warren Harding elected president; 19th Amendment (women's suffrage) ratified; union membership reaches 5 million

1922 – Fordney-McCumber Tariff passed

1923 – Harding dies in office and Vice President Calvin Coolidge becomes president

1924 – Coolidge elected president

1926 – Revenue Act cuts taxes and partially implements Treasury Secretary Andrew Mellon's "scientific taxation"

1928 – Republican Herbert Hoover elected president

1929 – Stock Market crashes; union membership decreases to less than 3 million; Agricultural Marketing Act enacted; White House Conference of Business held

1929 -1941 – The Great Depression

1930 – Hawley-Smoot Tariff passed; Federal Reserve Board eases credit; 1352 banks fail

1931 – National Credit Corporation established; 2294 banks fail

1932 – Hoover Administration establishes Reconstruction Finance Corporation; first Glass-Steagall Act enacted; Democrat Franklin D. Roosevelt elected president; cereal and cotton market prices fall to one-third of 1920 levels

1933 – Emergency Banking Act, Glass-Steagall Act, Agricultural Adjustment Act, National Industrial Recovery Act, and Securities Act all enacted; Public Works Administration and Tennessee Valley Authority established; corporate concentration increases, with 594 corporations owning 53 percent of all domestic assets

1934 – Securities Exchange Act, National Housing Act, and Gold Standard Act all enacted

1935 – Supreme Court decides Schechter Poultry Corp. v. United States; Social Security Act, Emergency Relief Act, Revenue Act, National Labor Relations Act, Public Utilities Holding Company Act, and Banking Act all enacted; Works Progress Administration established

1936 – Roosevelt reelected; Supreme Court decides United States v. Butler

1937 – Roosevelt announces "Court-Packing" Plan; Supreme Court decides West Coast Hotel v. Parrish and National Labor Relations Board v. Jones & Laughlin Steel Corp.

1937-1938 – "Roosevelt Recession"

1938 – Fair Labor Standards Act and revised Agricultural Adjustment Act enacted

1939 – Federal spending totals $9.4 billion

1939-1945 – Federal Budget increases 18 fold; GNP increases 2 ½ times

1940 – Roosevelt elected for a third term; Unemployment at 15 percent

1941 – Office of Scientific Research & Development created

1941-1945 – World War II fought; Costs of War at $300 billion; Federal Debt increases five fold

1942 – Pentagon built; Manhattan Project (Atomic Bomb) instituted; Supreme Court decides Wickard v. Filburn

1944 – Roosevelt reelected for a fourth term; one-half

of domestic productive capacity directed to war effort; unemployment sinks to one percent

1945 – Roosevelt dies; Two Atomic Bombs dropped on Japan; World War II ends; Vice President Harry Truman becomes president; Gross National Product reaches $200 billion; federal spending totals $95.2 billion

1947 – Taft-Hartley Act enacted; George Kennan's article "The Sources of Soviet Conduct" published in Foreign Affairs; first "Levittown" begun in Nassau County, New York

1950 – Korean War begins; NSC-68 issued; Federal spending totals $43.1 billion

1952 – Hydrogen Bomb developed; McDonald's begins licensing of its "Speedy Service System"

1953 – Federal spending totals $50.4 billion; Korean War Peace Treaty signed

1955 – General Motors becomes first American corporation with $1 billion in sales; Salk anti-polio vaccine introduced

1956 – Interstate Highway Act enacted

1957 – Gaither Report issued; Russia launches Sputnik satellite

1958 – National Aeronautics and Space Administration ("NASA") established

1961 – President Eisenhower gives Farewell Address warning of threats from military-industrial complex and technological revolution

INTRODUCTION

One of the firestorms which erupted during the 2012 presidential election came when the incumbent, President Barack Obama, told business, "You didn't build that," suggesting that government deserved the credit for business growth. Hard-working business people who had created their businesses through years of multiple economic and personal challenges with little or no pay, took umbrage at the president's comment. In fact, the relationship between business and government has been a vacillating one. At times and very much in a cyclical manner, government has alternated between advancing and constraining business growth and operations. For example, in the years following the Civil War through the end of the nineteenth century, friendly administrations, mainly Republican, financed the growth of railroads and sponsored other measures to build an integrated and protected national market for the products of American business. By contrast, in the first half of the twentieth century, Progressives and New Dealers placed business under increasing regulation not only to combat excesses but also to attempt to manage the economy in the place of private enterprise.

This book examines the interaction, at times cooperative, and at others confrontational, of government policy and business development in the crucial 100 year period between the onset of the Civil War in 1860 and the height of the Cold War in 1960. Our focus is directed at actions taken at the federal level of government because their impact has had the widest effect upon business, particularly in the twentieth century. Through oscillating and often inconsistent cycles of regulation and deregulation, a framework emerged over the time period covered in this work which permitted the United States to attain worldwide economic supremacy and leadership after World War II.

Chapter 1 documents how the Civil War ended the reign of the southern "Slave Power" in the federal government it had controlled to that time. Southern interests favored agriculture over industrial development, and hamstrung northern efforts to build an industrial economy which expanded across the entire American continent. With the secession of the South, northern interests were enabled finally to enact legislation to construct a transcontinental railroad network; to pass tariffs protective of American businesses; to establish a system of national banks; to set up homesteading programs to open up the West for settlement; and generally to advance the interests of American industry. As such, the Civil War cleared the path for the business-friendly initiatives of the federal government which followed for the remainder of the nineteenth century.

Chapter 2 examines the policies pursued by federal and state governments which, together with other factors, facilitated the tripling of the Gross National Product of the United States from 1865 to 1900. These policies included continuation of a tariff regime protective of American businesses, and massive federal and state funding of internal improvements, especially railroads, which permitted a unitary national market to develop. In addition, liberal immigration policies had the dual benefit of attracting workers, both skilled and unskilled, from Europe, as well as recruiting additional settlers to populate the Midwest and West. New inventions and technologies were also encouraged by the patent system, and an American System of manufacture emerged, perfecting both the uniformity and interchangeability of parts to permit more efficient production of goods. Finally, in order to prepare the western half of the United States for settlement, the federal government enacted a number of homestead laws, while also pursuing shameful policies which led to elimination or marginalization of the Native Americans who had lived there.

Chapters 3 and 4 document the initial cyclical change in governmental policy towards business. These chapters examine two movements which advocated a system of regulating business operations to replace the laissez-faire approach to business pursued by the federal and state governments in the last third of the nineteenth century. Chapter 3 reviews the Populist Movement, which originally arose out of an agrarian discontent which became focused both politically and socially through groups such as the Grangers and the Farmers' Alliances. The Populists sought to reform the monetary system to replace the tight money policies of the Republican administrations, which hurt the farming community, with a flexible national currency which included unlimited coinage of both silver and gold. The Populist Platform called for the abolition of national banks and of foreclosures on farms; sought nationalization of public utilities, including railroads, telephone, and telegraph facilities; and called for the formation of federal warehouses which would store and fund farmers' crops before their ultimate sale. The Populists were largely unsuccessful, particularly at the federal level, and faded from view after they joined forces with the Democratic Party of William Jennings Bryan, which lost the critical presidential election of 1896 to the business-oriented Republican, William McKinley.

Chapter 4 turns to the more successful Progressive Movement, which sought to implement reforms through a diverse coalition which included journalists and novelists; management experts and professional associations; women's groups; clergy in the Social Gospel Movement; and a mix of politicians who took different approaches to business reform and regulation. The Progressives sought legislatively to impose structure and order on society in general. With respect to business, their overall goal was to "give the government more power in business affairs," although the three Progressive presidents, Theodore Roosevelt, William Howard Taft, and Woodrow Wilson disagreed on how best to implement this goal. Roosevelt wanted to break up "bad" trusts, while facilitating the operations of those trusts he deemed to be "good." Taft relied more on enforcing the existing antitrust laws against all trusts. Wilson obtained enactment of "remedial legislation" to combat the predatory activities of large corporations, and established the Federal Trade Commission, with broad powers to ban "unfair methods of competition." To rationalize and to place the banking system on a sound footing, Wilson also was able to erect the Federal Reserve System.

Chapter 5 documents another cyclical change in the governmental approach to business, this time stemming initially from the needs of World War I, and thereafter from the return of Republican rule in the 1920s. The largely confrontational approach to business pursued by the Progressives was replaced by a cooperative and voluntary effort between government and business to meet the needs of the war economy. Multiple federal agencies were established to facilitate the war effort and to make business more efficient under the Democrat President Woodrow Wilson. The federal government, for example, took over and streamlined the railroad system, while also encouraging the growth of large corporations and shelving enforcement of the antitrust laws during the war. At the end of the war, the Republican Party was restored to power through 1932, and reverted to many of the business-friendly policies it had pursued in the nineteenth century. Protective tariffs were raised; taxes were decreased; the national debt was reduced; and business regulation was lessened. With a stock market crash in 1929, and a depression which followed, President Herbert Hoover continued a voluntary approach with business through multiple initiatives, none of which was successful in stemming the economic decline. In his most significant action, Hoover established the Reconstruction Finance Corporation, which became the first federal agency to directly intervene in the American economy during peacetime.

Chapter 6 discusses the transformational change from a largely unregulated business economy to an administrative, regulatory state under President Franklin Roosevelt's three sequential New Deals. While never following a consistent policy approach, Roosevelt regularly expanded the power of the federal government and imposed federal regulation on most sectors of the economy, including agriculture, aviation, banking, communications, electric power, housing, labor relations, and securities transactions. His First New Deal separated commercial and investment banking, gave the federal banking authorities power to inspect and regulate banks, and established a system of deposit insurance. Agriculture was regulated, with farmers paid not to grow crops, and business was empowered, under government supervision, to establish "codes of fair competition" to regulate prices and production, while adhering to fair labor standards. In a Second New Deal, the Roosevelt Administration enacted relief legislation, including the historic Social Security Act, and established the Works Progress

Administration to supplement the Public Works Administration of the First New Deal. The Second New Deal also established a national labor board to mandate collective bargaining, to compel union recognition, and to issue cease and desist orders, while the Public Utilities Holding Company Act restricted the activities of utilities, and subjected them to continuing regulation, including the compelled divestiture of certain assets. A weakened Third New Deal was only able to secure enactment of the Fair Labor Standards Act of 1938, which prescribed a maximum workweek of 40 hours and a minimum hourly wage for most non-agricultural businesses. Taken as a whole, the Roosevelt presidencies birthed a regulatory state through which a myriad of federal agencies still promulgate detailed regulations prescribing precise parameters under which businesses are mandated to conduct their affairs.

Chapter 7 outlines the significant impacts that World War II and the Cold War had on American business, including the birth of "Pentagon Capitalism." Business was a major beneficiary of a war economy which cost over $300 billion to run, and GNP increased two and one-half times from 1939 to 1945. Induced by tax breaks, low interest loans, lucrative cost-plus contracts, and a dampening of antitrust enforcement, business shifted its productive capacity from consumer goods to war materials. With funds largely provided by the newly-established Office of Scientific Research and Development, American business and universities also sparked advancements in such areas as electronics, telecommunications, synthetic materials, drugs, medical equipment, radar, and airplane and ship design. The most significant scientific accomplishment was the development of the atomic bomb, which required expenditures of $2 billion, and the work of over 125,000 individuals.

The Cold War had a further expansive impact on American business, leading to the emergence of a military-industrial economy fostered by government spending. From 1945 to 1960, the Gross National Product of the country grew from $200 billion to $500 billion in a post World War II economic boom. A "Baby Boom" was a contributing factor which increased business markets, especially in children's products, and a significant shift of population to suburban areas took place, fostered by a new interstate highway system. Huge increases in defense spending further entrenched Pentagon Capitalism, and federal funding of research and development in defense and related industries led to the development of a host of new products, including transistors, and new industries, including computers. These developments led President Dwight D. Eisenhower prophetically to warn of the emergence of both a "military-industrial complex" which could gain unwarranted influence on public affairs, and a technological revolution which posed the danger that "public policy could…become the captive of a scientific-technological elite."

In the Conclusion, we analyze five recurring patterns in the relationship between business and government from 1860 to 1960, and which continue to the present. First, there have been cycles alternating between deregulation and regulation, sometimes advancing, while at other times retarding, business growth. Second, government has played a vital role in assisting business by funding infrastructure expansion. Third, war and other conflicts from the Civil War through the Cold War to the War on Terror have created new markets and birthed new technologies which have fueled business growth. Fourth, government has promoted and safeguarded business innovation through government funding of research and development and also through a series of laws, including protections granted to patents, copyrights, and trade secrets. Fifth, access to the judicial system has provided business with a safety valve to employ against overly restrictive regulation.

CHAPTER ONE
CRUSHING THE SLAVE POWER

The Civil War was the defining event of the nineteenth century in the United States, and its effects radiate into the twenty-first. Clearing obstacles to developing a new industrial economy and eliminating slavery came at a great price. The sorrowful statistics of the war dead record the greatest sacrifice. Recent, census-based counts of the war dead place the figure in excess of 750,000 killed in battle, more than all of the individuals who died in every other war fought by Americans until the late twentieth century. One out of every ten men who was of military age in 1860 was dead by the war's end five years later. In the South, the stark fact of death claimed one of every four who fought for the Confederacy. On one day alone – September 17, 1862 – at Antietam Creek in Maryland, more than 6000 died or were fatally wounded. This carnage totaled twice the number killed in the terrorist attacks on the World Trade Center in New York on September 11, 2001, from an

1862 population one-eighth the size of that of 2001. And on both sides, Union and Confederate, far too many of those who survived lived out their remaining lives with lost limbs and broken spirits.

Beyond the human cost, the economy of the South was literally torn apart. Much of the southern railroad network was blown up, both track and bridges. More than 50 percent of the farm machinery in the South was destroyed, and 40 percent of its livestock was killed. As a result, the southern share of total American wealth declined from 30 percent in 1860 to 12 percent in 1870.

What caused this great war? And *how* did it do so?

While slavery is the common answer, single-explanation theories mirror the use of exaggerated perspective in art. By emphasizing a particular feature, they focus such attention upon it that they tend to exclude or minimize other important factors. The slavery explanation often suffers from such exaggeration. Abraham Lincoln knew this. In his Second Inaugural Address, he sagely observed that "All knew that this [slave] interest was, somehow, the cause of the war."

"Somehow" is the key word, recognizing the subtlety of the inquiry. Lincoln, a skilled trial lawyer before he assumed the presidency, knew that lawyers and judges recognize that multiple causes can exist to explain a particular event, each being a "substantial factor" in bringing about a result for which an actor may properly be held responsible. This was the case with the Civil War.

In this chapter we focus upon two of the factors which led to civil war because they also impeded the growth of an industrial economy in the United States in the mid-nineteenth century. These two factors were, first, the social and economic differences between the North and South, and, second, the disproportionate political power of the South. This analysis is not meant to suggest that these factors, by themselves, explain the outbreak of the Civil War in the United States in 1860. They do not.

Regional Social and Economic Differences

By 1860, the North and South were economically two different nations, each successful in its own sphere. The North was mainly industrial with a large labor force in its cities. The South was nearly all agricultural and rural. By 1860, the percentage of Northerners engaged in agriculture had declined from the turn of the century from 68 to 40 percent. In the same period, the percentage of Southerners which engaged in agriculture actually increased, from 82 to 84 percent. With 42 percent of the nation's population in 1860, the South had only 16 percent of its manufacturing capacity, a decrease of four percent from 1840. Larger towns were also more common in the North; twenty percent of all Northerners in 1850 lived in towns with populations over 2500. By contrast, only eight percent in the South (2.5 percent in the lower South) lived in towns of this size.

The economic ties that previously provided some bonds between North and South were also loosened by the emergence at the mid-nineteenth century of what Marc Egnal has termed the "Lake Economy," which linked producers and consumers in parts of the North and the Midwest through transportation on the Great

Lakes and through the Erie Canal, all at the expense of Southern economic interests. The 1850s also saw the rise of explicitly sectional parties in the North, culminating with the emergence of the Republican Party, which ran its first candidate for president, John C. Fremont, in 1856. Fremont ran on a platform which called for "Free Soil" and "Free Men," and won all of New England and New York, along with the Midwest states of Iowa, Michigan, Ohio, and Wisconsin. This electoral North-South split divided the sections further, and posed an economic threat to the continued national legislative dominance of the "Slave Power" of the South and its Southern Planter pseudo aristocracy, a point discussed further below.

Differences in economics were aggravated by regional differences in attitudes about those economics. "The Cotton Kingdom" saw itself as superior both morally and culturally to Northern merchants and the forces of "free labor." Lincoln spoke the gospel of free labor, explaining how men progress through their own hard work. Notably, it was not on the backs of others. Instead, the individual laborer would slowly improve his position in society. "The man who labored for another last year, this year labors for himself, and next year he will hire others to labor for him."

By contrast, the planters of the South adopted Jefferson's harsh views of labor. In his *Notes on the State of Virginia*, written in the early 1780s, Jefferson proclaimed that "Those who labor in the earth are the chosen people of God, if ever he had a chosen people, whose breasts he has made his particular deposit for substantial and genuine virtue." By contrast, Jefferson continued, "the mobs of great cities add just so much to the support of pure government, as sores do to the strength of the human body." From this he concluded that "While we have land to labour then, let us never wish to see our citizens occupied at a work-bench, or twirling a distaff."

This view of Lincoln's free laborers as infectious agents in the body politic remained a major theme in mid-nineteenth century Southern history. As a former Texas Senator put it, "We are an agricultural people... We have no cities – we don't want them...We want no manufactures: we desire no trading, no mechanical or manufacturing classes." Indeed, in his inaugural address, President Jefferson Davis of the Confederate States of America proclaimed that the South was "an agricultural people, whose chief interest is the export of commodities required in every manufacturing country."

Southern opposition to measures friendly to the development of an industrial economy mired the economic development of the United States in decades of political stalemate. High on the list of Southern opposition were protective tariffs and a national bank, both measures which sought to implement the Hamiltonian vision of a mercantile America. The tariff issue emerged in a serious political war between the states in 1828, with the so-called "Tariff of Abominations." The political fight which ensued brought forth the southern intellectual defense of its states' rights philosophy in John C. Calhoun's *South Carolina Exposition and Protest*, which was augmented in his Ford Hill Address of 1831. Calhoun was

Andrew Jackson's vice president and a nationalist, but one who believed that the rights of substantial minority interests must be protected by the national government. He evolved the concept of "concurrent majorities," under which it was necessary for the government to protect minority interests by obtaining their assent to major political decisions in order to preserve the legitimacy of rule by a mere numerical majority. Calhoun would have therefore required the legislatures of each state to give their assent to any law with nationwide impact before it could take effect, granting the South a veto over laws which would further Northern economic interests.

When the tariff issue failed to subside and Congress amended the tariff in 1832 in order to assist Northern industrial interests, South Carolina – which later would become the first state to secede from the Union – called a Convention which passed an Ordinance of Nullification on November 24, 1832, declaring the 1828 and 1832 tariffs unconstitutional and prohibiting collection of the tariff duties within the state. Calhoun resigned as vice president, and sabers were rattled, only to be resheathed when President Andrew Jackson threatened to send in federal troops and hang for treason those who interfered with the collection of tariff duties. Finally, Henry Clay proposed a successful political solution through a compromise tariff, and the immediate threat ended.

At the same time as the nullification controversy was developing, fault lines directly linked to slavery began to appear within the fifteen slave states themselves. As William W. Freehling has documented, slavery had become compressed within the seven lower Southern states. Those states (in order of their later secession from the Union) – South Carolina, Mississippi, Florida, Alabama, Georgia, Louisiana, and Texas – had a slave population of some 47 percent. Significantly, these were the states most opposed to measures which aided Northern commercial expansion. They all left the Union after Lincoln was elected, but before he took office.

By contrast to the states in the lower South, the upper- and mid-South states of Virginia, Arkansas, Tennessee, and North Carolina had a slave population of only 32 percent. They seceded after Lincoln's inauguration and only after the Civil War had begun at Fort Sumter. Trailing in the rear were the four border slave states, none of which seceded from the Union. In those states of Maryland, Delaware, Missouri, and Kentucky, the slave population was only 14 percent. Significantly, the further north a state was located, the less opposed it was as a general matter to Northern business interests. Moreover, even in the upper South, there was considerable support for the North and for economic development among the non-slaveholder classes.

Some Southern leaders, particularly in the lower South, were fearful that slavery would die unless it expanded. They inflamed Northern abolitionists by calling for several measures. First, with little support, they sought to legalize the African slave trade, which had been barred by Congress in 1807. Second, they attempted to expand the slave domain southward, principally into Cuba. The 1860 federal census counted nearly 4,000,000 slaves in the South; Cuba alone would add another 500,000. Two significant efforts were made to acquire Cuba under the administrations of Presidents James Polk and Franklin Pierce in 1847 and 1852, with offers made to Spain to sell Cuba for sums of $100 million and higher. When these offers were rejected, President Pierce considered a Bay-of-Pigs-like plan to incite a revolution in Cuba in 1852. Two years later, a secret memorandum was sent to Pierce by several American diplomats, who called for seizing Cuba by force if Spain continued to refuse to sell the island. Known to history as the Ostend Manifesto, from the Belgian town in which the diplomats met, its signatories included James Buchanan, who shortly would become president, but was then serving as minister to Great Britain.

A third measure was the most incendiary, inflaming Northern interests well beyond those represented by the abolitionists. This was the Kansas-Nebraska Act of 1854, which permitted the expansion of slavery into new territories if the resident voters so chose. As such, it repudiated the Missouri Compromise of 1820, and threatened to bring slavery into the North. The expectation was that Kansas would be a slave state, and Nebraska, a free state. Both sides rushed settlers into Kansas, and widespread violence soon spawned the name "Bleeding Kansas." It was in Kansas that John Brown began his biblically-tinged type of terrorism, butchering with broadswords five pro-slavery settlers in May of 1856. When Senator Charles Sumner of Massachusetts took the Senate floor in 1856 to attack the South for its part in the Kansas violence, South Carolina Representative Preston Brooks caned him nearly to death for assailing his cousin, Senator

Andrew Butler, and for comparing support for slavery to the love of a prostitute. Censured by the House, Brooks resigned, only to be reelected back home by a large majority.

The Kansas-Nebraska Act brought Abraham Lincoln back into politics, while also dealing a death blow to his Whig Party, which had stood for national expansion, protective tariffs, and a system of internal improvements which would tie the separate sections of the country together economically. The demise of the Whigs was an act of creative destruction politically, for it sowed the seeds for the emergence two years later of the (eventually) more successful Republican Party, which went on to implement much of the Whig's economic program.

In 1854, Lincoln began his campaign against the extension of slavery beyond the South, characterizing the Kansas-Nebraska Act as a "moral wrong," and observing that "The spirit of seventy-six and the spirit of Nebraska are utter antagonisms... Our republican robe is soiled, and trailed in the dust. Let us repurify it."

Repurification was not an option. Instead, violence continued, with dueling votes and vote fraud in Kansas, leading to the notorious pro-slavery Lecompton Constitution being passed by the United States Senate, but narrowly defeated in the House of Representatives. That Constitution would have led to Kansas being admitted as a slave state in 1858.

These attempts to expand slavery in the 1850s had another divisive consequence because they also caused Northern whites to fear the further growth of the already significant Southern political power, with a consequent threat to their own civil liberties and economic interests. As Michael Woods has put it, "The slave power was defined not by racism but by slaveholders' capacity to use federal law and muscle to advance their class interests."

Regional Legal Differences

Law often follows economics, and this was the case in nineteenth-century America. Because of the shift to a mercantile economy in the North in the mid-nineteenth century, legal doctrines which inhibited the growth of new businesses were discarded in favor of new doctrines which protected nascent industries from the threat of ruinous liability. In the law of contracts, for example, the hoary maxim that a sound price demanded a sound commodity threatened endless litigation over sales made by middlemen, when ultimate purchasers questioned the fairness of the exchanges from their rear view windows. As a result, courts began to employ a different approach in determining what was necessary to uphold a contract. This became known as the "will" theory of contract, under which the relevant inquiry was not the *fairness* of the exchange, but rather whether there was *mutual assent*, accompanied by *some consideration*. The doctrine of caveat emptor emerged to protect market transactions, granting them the necessary finality.

Decisions of the Supreme Court of the United States often favored this mercantile view even before the onset of the Civil War under both Chief Justice John Marshall, a Federalist, and Chief Justice Roger Taney, a Jacksonian Democrat. An early example was the famous case of *Charles River Bridge v. Warren Bridge*

(1837). There, in upholding the rights of the owners of a new bridge to build their bridge across the Charles River in Massachusetts over the objections of the proprietors of an existing bridge which had possessed a monopoly over bridge traffic in the area, the court recognized the imperatives of business expansion. Thus, in ruling in favor of the new entrant by a bare four to three vote, the court majority, speaking through Taney, relied upon the fact that "new channels of communication are daily found necessary, both for travel and trade, and are essential to the comfort, convenience, and prosperity of the people." As such, to foreclose new entrants would be to invite older forms of transportation to "call...upon this court to put down the improvements which have taken their place." That was unacceptable because it would take a nation that was "free, active, and enterprising, continually advancing in numbers and wealth," and throw it "back to the improvements of the last century... [and] obliged to stand still."

Similarly, in *Bank of Augusta v. Earle* (1839), while bowing to states' rights in theory, the Supreme Court struck down state-imposed restrictions on the right of out-of-state banks to sue on negotiable instruments, assuring that the channels of interstate commerce would be open to foreign businesses. Most significantly, in *Swift v. Tyson* (1842), a unanimous Supreme Court overturned a New York court's interpretation of that state's law of negotiable instruments which had rendered the bill of exchange involved in that case defective and thus unenforceable. Citing the need for uniformity in "questions of general commercial law," the court began its construction of a federal common law which would govern questions commercial law for the next 96 years, until it was finally overruled by the decision in *Erie Railroad Co. v. Tompkins* (1938).

The Supreme Court's capacious approach to accommodating business interests was followed by many Northern courts. These courts sought to favor corporate development by formulating legal rules which lessened liability to injured workers. Replacing what was often a legal regime of strict liability for such injuries, Northern courts developed a series of legal doctrines to require proof of fault through employer negligence before liability could be imposed upon their corporate enterprises. Additional doctrines, which soon became received wisdom, emerged to further limit worker recoveries. These included contributory negligence, which foreclosed any recovery by injured employees if they were partially at fault; assumption of the risk; and the "fellow servant" rule. This latter doctrine provided that an injured worker's legal remedy was to be found against a co-worker, rather than the employer, where the co-worker was the immediate cause of the injury. Rules barring recovery on narrowed views of legal causation also protected corporations, as did procedural reforms giving courts more power to take cases from juries, or to set aside their verdicts if those verdicts were considered by the trial or appellate judge to be "contrary to the weight of the evidence."

By contrast to these business-friendly Northern courts, courts in the lower South, where slavery was most concentrated, rejected some of these novel legal theories. In the law of contract, for example, these courts continued to apply the theory that a "sound price" required provision of a "sound commodity." This theory was important in states where slavery existed, because of the great expenditures required to purchase slaves and the corresponding catastrophic impact upon a planter if he paid too high a price for a slave who was physically or mentally impaired, and was thus unable to work the long hours necessary to advance the economics of the Cotton Kingdom in those states. While some states like Louisiana handled these matters through detailed statutes regulating the slave trade, most Southern states relied upon the courts to fashion appropriate common law rules and regulation over that trade. These typically favored the purchaser of a slave, protecting him from a deceitful seller without imposing any concept of caveat emptor. Indeed, some courts in the lower South even held that an implied warranty was given by the seller of the slave relating to the slave's fitness for the work of the purchaser.

In the area of tort law, most Southern courts declined to apply the fellow servant rule to slaves. This was because the master would become responsible for paying any judgment imposed because of the slave's negligent conduct which harmed a fellow worker. The issue was most important where a slave was hired out by the slave owner to an independent business enterprise, which happened with some frequency. Indeed, conservative estimates suggest that more than five percent of slaves worked in industrial occupations before the Civil War. To avoid the master being saddled with any award of damages resulting from the slave's work, Southern courts continued to hold the enterprise, rather than the master, liable, rejecting the fellow servant rule.

This growing divergence in legal doctrine between North and South posed a problem to emerging business interests and served as a disincentive to entry into Southern commerce by Northern corporate entities. Thus, economic differences between a North which was becoming more commercial, and a South which was remaining staunchly agricultural and slave-supported, particularly in the seven states of the Lower South, were reflected in how the law developed differently in the two areas. Once again, the house was divided.

Disproportionate Southern Political Power

Northerners in the nineteenth century increasingly resented what became known as the "Slave Power." With only approximately one-third of the nation's population in 1860, the South had nevertheless controlled every branch of the federal government from its formation in 1789 to the outbreak of civil war in 1861. During this period, seven of the 13 presidents (serving for 47 of the 71 years in this period) and 19 of the 34 Supreme Court justices were southerners, and often slave owners as well. Two of every three Presidents Pro Tem of the Senate and Speakers of the House were also southerners during these years.

Part of the South's political power came from Article 1, Section 2 of the Constitution, which counted slaves both in awarding seats in the House of Representatives and in fixing the number of presidential electors. Thus, slaves, who were considered to be chattels like furniture for every other purpose, were counted as three-fifths of a person for political representation under the Constitution. It was provisions such as these which led the abolitionist William Lloyd Garrison to damn the Constitution as "a covenant with death, and an agreement with hell."

The South used its political power to block Northern commercial interests. We have already seen how, in the 1830s, the issue of protective tariffs for Northern industry led to Southern theories of nullification, concurrent majorities, and threats of secession. Under the presidency of Democrat James Polk, a Southerner, protective tariffs were ended by the Walker Tariff in 1845, which remained in force until the Panic of 1857 devastated the Northern economy. So serious was the tariff question for the South that the Constitution of the Confederacy explicitly barred the use of protective tariffs in the seceded states.

Another issue on which the South was able to block northern economic interests was the question of the existence of a national bank. Ruled constitutional in the seminal decision in *McCulloch v. Maryland* (1819), which adopted the expansive Hamiltonian view of the Necessary and Proper Clause of the Constitution in place of Jefferson's more narrow focus, the recharter of the Bank of the United States was nevertheless struck down in 1832, in a veto message written for President Andrew Jackson by his attorney general, Roger Taney. That veto message characterized the bank as an instrument of a powerful mercantile clique of "the rich and powerful," which was aligned with foreign interests, all conspiring against the interests of "the humble members of society -- the farmers, mechanics and laborers...."

Striking down the national bank also permitted increased power over currency decisions at the state level. The national bank had pursued a mercantile policy of a strong, deflated currency, which favored creditors over debtors by assuring that creditors were repaid in currency which retained its full value, rather than currency which was worth less in real terms because inflation had lowered the purchasing power of that currency. Thus, a lender extending a $1000 loan which would purchase ten bushels of wheat at the time of the loan should be repaid that sum in dollars which maintained the power to purchase the same (or even more) number of bushels.

By contrast to the national bank's deflationary policy, the Jacksonian Democrats and their southern adherents generally favored a cheaper currency to advance their own economic interests. Their desire was, for example, to borrow $1000 in 1845 and repay that amount in 1855 in inflated dollars worth only $800 compared to the original purchasing power in 1845.

Under Taney as chief justice, the Supreme Court implemented this southern approach before the the Civil War in cases such as *Briscoe v. Bank of Kentucky* (1837), which ruled that Article I, Section 10 of the Constitution, which barred states from issuing bills of credit, did not prohibit a state-chartered and state-owned bank from issuing negotiable notes. Such notes increased the money supply, and thus advanced southern interests over those of the "sound money" policies of northern capitalists. President Jackson saw those policies of Nicholas Biddle and his Second Bank of the United States as having precipitated the Panic of 1819, and President Polk continued the Jacksonian policy in the banking area, minimizing the federal role, and expanding that of the states.

Other areas in which the South was politically able to block northern economic interests included the construction of a transcontinental railroad; financing of internal improvements such as roads, canals, and the dredging of harbors (the latter being vital for the expansion of the Lake Economy mentioned above); and the encouragement of homesteading in the West. In the case of the transcontinental railroad, the South stymied Northern efforts to authorize construction of such a railroad from 1848 on because it believed that it would be politically disadvantaged if a northern or central route were chosen. Not able to command a majority for a southern route, the "Slave Power" could nevertheless block any northern route, and it did so until outbreak of the Civil War.

Internal improvements were also seen by Southern interests as designed to aid Northern commerce at a great cost to the federal government, which in turn threatened higher tariffs to generate revenue to pay these increased costs. Finally, the South opposed homesteading initiatives in the West because it believed that such efforts would lead to the creation of more free states when the population in the West became sufficiently large to justify statehood.

Given the political deadlock between North and

South in the two decades before civil war broke out, the expansion of a market economy to the Pacific Ocean was stymied before 1860.

Each of these factors divided North from South, and each was exacerbated by a series of political measures taken in the 1850s. J. G. Randall has called the political leaders of this decade "the blundering generation." In his view, weak and misguided presidents from the Whigs Zachary Taylor and Millard Fillmore through the Democrats Franklin Pierce and James Buchanan, aided and abetted by Roger Taney's Supreme Court and southern political leaders, took a series of ill-considered steps which threatened to make slavery national and placed a spotlight on the attempts to extend the reach of the "Slave Power."

Without accepting Randall's characterization of the political and judicial leaders who were responsible for them, there were three developments which in fact further exacerbated the division of North from South in the 1850s. The major irritants were the Fugitive Slave Law enacted as part of the Compromise of 1850; the Kansas-Nebraska Act of 1854; and the Supreme Court's 1857 decision in the *Dred Scott* case.

Before 1850, there were 15 free and 15 slave states, a balance that ensured the continuance of the Slave Power if additional free states were not admitted. Texas had become a slave state, admitted through annexation in 1845 with the right to split into five separate states. With the Mexican War then threatening to add even more slave states, the House of Representatives twice passed Pennsylvania Representative David Wilmot's

Bill which would have banned slavery in any territory taken from Mexico. In 1846, and again in 1847, the Senate, which was equally divided between free and slave states, rejected this so-called "Wilmot Proviso." This rejection sparked creation of the Free Soil Party, which ran former President Martin Van Buren as its candidate in 1848, an election in which he received over ten percent of the total popular vote.

By 1850, the need to act on the status of the territories acquired from Mexico resulted in the Compromise of 1850. Its most significant provisions were the admission of California as a free state, giving a one-state majority to the free states; no restrictions prohibiting slavery being placed on the territories of New Mexico and Utah; and a new and savage Fugitive Slave Law. Daniel Webster, then at the end of his long political career, fought for passage of the Compromise, urging that the Union be preserved. Opposing him was Senator William Seward of New York, who invoked a "higher law," and would later speak of an "irrepressible conflict" between North and South.

The Fugitive Slave Law was enacted with harsh penalties. These included a $1000 fine and a $1000 civil damages award against any person who aided an escaped slave, as well as a prison term of up to six months for such individuals. In addition, if the federal commissioner found the person before him to be a slave, he received ten dollars; if he ruled in the accused's favor, he received only five dollars.

A few highly visible cases involving escaped slaves ignited abolitionist sentiments in the North, converting many who had been neutral before to the cause. In reality, this was the most significant effect of the Fugitive Slave Law of 1850, because less than 350 purported slaves were processed under the provisions of law in the entire decade that followed its enactment.

To combat the opposition to enforcement of the Fugitive Slave Law, and to preserve the Union, Daniel Webster called for treason trials for those who opposed enforcement of that law. The trials soon came, after a southern slave owner seeking to recapture two escaped slaves was killed, along with his son, in a riot in Christiana, Pennsylvania, on September 11, 1851. Following this incident, President Fillmore sent in the Marines, and 36 black and five white men were indicted for treason. In the first trial, *United States v. Hanway* (1851), Justice Robert Grier of the Supreme Court, sitting as a trial judge, found that even forcible opposition to enforcement of the Fugitive Slave Law did not constitute treason, and the other cases were soon dropped. Nevertheless, as one abolitionist put it in a private letter, "These Treason Trials have been a great windfall" by stirring up additional Northern opposition to slavery.

If the Fugitive Slave Act of 1850 permitted the Slave Power to enter northern territory with a legal license to drag human beings from Northern freedom back into Southern slavery, the Kansas-Nebraska Act of 1854 threatened to bring slavery itself to the North, again under legal license. As already noted, Abraham Lincoln saw this as a stain on the Republican form of government, and most Northerners viewed the Act as a raw exercise of Southern political power which had to be opposed. Kansas thus became a literal and figurative battleground, with bloodshed on both sides, accompanied by further political savagery. This legislation thus added to the emotional division of North and South, paving the way for the future Civil War less than seven years later.

The third major political blunder of the 1850s was the Supreme Court's decision in *Scott v. Sandford* (1857). There, in a confusing witches' brew of nine separate opinions, the court ruled first that the Missouri Compromise of 1820, which drew a line across the country to ban slavery north of its boundary, was unconstitutional because Congress lacked power to ban slavery in the territories. It next concluded that slaves were property which could not be taken from their owners without due process of law. Taney's own opinion further outraged many Americans by ruling that blacks could not be citizens of the United States with the right to sue in federal court because they were considered in 1787 to be "a subordinate and inferior class of beings who had been subjugated by the dominant race, and, whether emancipated or not, yet remained subject to their authority, and had no rights or privileges but such as those who held the power and the Government might choose to grant them." Indeed, in this supposed popular view, blacks were "regarded as beings of an inferior order, and altogether unfit to associate with the white race." As such, "they have no rights which the white man was bound to respect."

Review of the private correspondence of the justices with president-elect Buchanan reveals how the

Dred Scott disposition came about, and lends some credence to the charge made by Lincoln in his June 16, 1858 "House Divided" speech that the presidency and the Supreme Court had acted in "pre-concert" upon "a common *plan*." Initially, the court had only intended to hold, consistent with earlier precedent, that the Missouri court ruling on Scott's status was binding, and to avoid any broader ruling, with its inevitable polarizing impact. Buchanan, however, sparked a different approach when he wrote to his old friend, Justice John Catron of Tennessee, to inquire when the decision would come down, so that he could incorporate it in his inaugural address. He went on to add that the Supreme Court should "destroy the dangerous slavery agitation and thus restore peace to our distracted country."

Catron wrote back that the case would be decided before the inauguration, but would "settle nothing," because it would not reach the issue of the validity of the Missouri Compromise. Less than two weeks later, Catron wrote another letter, now announcing that the court would reach that issue, and urging Buchanan to pressure his fellow Pennsylvanian, Justice Robert Grier, both to support the proposal of Justice Wayne of Georgia to write a broader opinion, and to join in it. Buchanan did so, and Grier promised, after speaking with Taney, to support the chief justice on the Missouri Compromise issue. He did so because he was "anxious that it should not appear that the line of latitude should mark the line of division in the court." Grier's vote led to an opinion which ruled against Scott's freedom.

Armed with this inside information, Buchanan

announced in his inaugural address that the issue of "when the people of a territory shall decide this [slavery] question for themselves" was then before the Supreme Court and "will, it is understood, be speedily and finally settled." He then added that "To their decision, in common with all good citizens, I shall cheerfully submit, *whatever [the decision] may be.*"

Of course, Buchanan knew what the decision *would* be, and it was announced publicly two days after his inauguration.

The *Dred Scott* decision met with violent opposition in the North, and further divided North from South. Many in the North and South believed that legalization of slavery in all states and territories would follow. As such, angry editorials and articles appeared in the North, denouncing the decision rendered by a court with a majority of Southern justices.

The authority of the Supreme Court began seriously to erode, so that two years later, the court's unanimous decision in *Ableman v. Booth* (1859), which upheld the conviction of an abolitionist editor under the Fugitive Slave Act for aiding the escape from jail of a slave, was defied by the Wisconsin courts and legislature. In response to the Supreme Court's dictum that the Fugitive Slave Act was "in all its provisions, fully authorized by the Constitution of the United States," the Wisconsin legislature called for "positive defiance" by the states against what it termed an "arbitrary act of power" in the ruling.

From the Compromise of 1850 to the Kansas-Nebraska Act of 1854 through the *Dred Scott* decision, the Slave Power overplayed its political hand, further polarizing the country into a downward spiral of mutual enmity, and separating political parties into increasingly sectional groupings.

Because slavery proved to be an intractable issue politically from 1830 to 1860, the existing party system of Whigs and Democrats increasingly fractionalized, leading to the disappearance of the Whig Party (the Party of Abraham Lincoln and his "beau ideal," Henry Clay) after the 1852 presidential election. The Democratic Party thereafter itself splintered into Northern and Southern branches in 1860.

Even before these developments, the existing political system was gradually disintegrating over a period of some twenty years, in several discrete steps. In 1840, the Liberty Party emerged, calling for the abolition of slavery by constitutional amendment. Its candidate for president, James Birney, received less than one percent of the popular vote for president in 1840, increasing to 2.3 percent in 1844.

By 1848, another new party emerged, expanding the base of the Liberty Party and absorbing most of its members. This "Free-Soil" Party included the so-called "Barnburners" who left the Democratic Convention in 1848, and also numbered among their ranks Charles Francis Adams, the son and grandson of presidents. Its rallying cry was "Free Soil, Free Labor, and Free Men." In 1848, its candidate was the former president, Martin Van Buren, who received 10.1 percent of the popular vote that year. That vote declined to five percent in 1852.

The Free Soilers, accompanied by "Conscience

Whigs" and abolitionist Democrats, soon transmuted into Republicans, yet another new political party formed in 1854. Their candidate, John C. Fremont, polled one-third of the popular vote for president in 1856, paving the way for Lincoln's election in 1860. In a four-way race, Lincoln took 39.8 percent of the popular vote. Stephen Douglas, the Northern Democratic candidate polled 29.5 percent, while John Breckinridge, Buchanan's vice president and the Southern Democratic candidate, took 18.1 percent. The fourth candidate, John Bell of the Union Party, trailed with 12.6 percent of the popular vote.

Lincoln carried every free state in 1860. Breckinridge took all of the lower South, while Bell won Tennessee (his home state), Virginia, and Kentucky. Douglas carried only the border state of Missouri. As of 1860, the politics of the soon-to-be-split nation were now fully sectional.

Effects of the Civil War on Future Economic Development

As Walter Licht has argued, it would be mistaken to explain the future growth of American industry as attributable to the Civil War itself. Nevertheless, the war served quickly to burn away obstacles to that growth by crushing the Slave Power and negating its effective veto on governmental measures to encourage business development. Thus, following the Civil War, Southern political power vanished during the remainder of the nineteenth century and well into the twentieth. The presidency was exclusively taken by Northerners until Woodrow Wilson's election in 1912, and by then, Wilson was a relocated Southerner, having moved from Virginia to New Jersey, where he served as president of Princeton University and as Governor of New Jersey. No Southerner served as Speaker of the House in the post-Civil-War nineteenth century, while only five of the 26 Supreme Court justices appointed and confirmed in the 50 years after the war came from the South.

After the initial secession of the lower Southern states, Congress was able to enact business-friendly legislation which had been defeated on previous attempts by Southern opposition. In 1861, tariffs protective of certain Northern businesses, including iron and coal producers, were enacted in the Morrill Tariff legislation. This was followed in 1862 by three major pieces of legislation. First came the enactment of the long-delayed Homestead Act which had been defeated by one vote in the Senate in 1858 and then was passed in 1859, but vetoed by President Buchanan. The 1862 Act granted up to 160 acres to settlers of Western public lands provided only that they remained on the land for five years and farmed it. Alternatively, these public lands could be purchased by settlers after six months for $1.25 an acre.

The second major piece of legislation enacted in 1862 was the Pacific Railway Act. This legislation finally set the stage for a transcontinental railroad, authorizing the construction of a north-central route from Omaha, Nebraska to Sacramento, California, funded by federal subsidies in the form of both money and land grants. Two railroads were involved in this massive construction effort. The Union Pacific Railroad was responsible for the construction from Kansas to Utah, while the Central Pacific Railroad built eastward from California to Utah. Construction began in 1865 and the two railroads met in May of 1869 in Utah, when the tracks were connected with the famous "Golden Spike."

Third, the Morrill Act of 1862 provided land grants to the states to establish colleges which would teach courses "related to agriculture and the mechanical arts." This began the system of land-grant colleges which today number over 100 in the United States and its territories. While generally thought to be oriented to agriculture, in fact these colleges also instructed students in scientific methods helpful to industrial development. These land-grant colleges included the Massachusetts Institute of Technology, the University of California at Berkeley, Cornell University, Purdue University, and the Universities of Florida, Georgia, Kentucky, Maine, Maryland, Tennessee, and Wisconsin.

These significant legislative accomplishments in 1862 were followed in 1863 by the enactment of a National Bank Act. This legislation permitted state banks to become national banks by buying United States bonds equal in amount to one-third of the state bank's paid-in capital stock, and establishing reserves against both bank notes and deposit liabilities. While few state banks converted in the early years, eventually a parallel system of national and state banks emerged and continues to this day.

CHAPTER TWO

THE ASCENT OF BUSINESS:
FUELING ECONOMIC DEVELOPMENT

The last third of the nineteenth century was a decisive period for the economic development of the United States. From the end of the Civil War in 1865 to the turn of the century in 1900, the population of the country nearly doubled from approximately 40 million to more than 75 million, while the Gross National Product of the United States increased threefold. By 1900, the United States was the largest manufacturing country in the world, producing 30 percent of all manufactured goods. Nearly 25 percent of the workforce was engaged in industry. As manufacturing grew in all areas of the country, agriculture did as well. In the West, for example, farming and cattle ranching were key components in settling the country west of the Mississippi. Large scale or "factory farming" emerged with tenant farmers operating lands owned by absentee speculators.

The expansion of manufacturing and agricultural

enterprises throughout the country in the last third of the nineteenth century is attributable in major part to explicit pro-business policies adopted by the predominantly Republican administrations which governed during that period. These policies included:

- protective tariffs,
- funding of internal improvements, especially in transportation,
- liberal immigration laws, which produced a workforce to build the nation, as well as settlers for the West,
- the grant of patents, and the encouragement of new technology, and
- development of the West, with the addition of eight new states by 1890.

In this chapter, we first review how these policies assisted in the expansion of the industrial economy, particularly in the East, Midwest and South. Second, we see how the development of the lands west of the Mississippi River was aided by governmental and private initiatives.

<u>The Growth of the Industrial Economy</u>

In the period following the Civil War, there were major manufacturing centers throughout the country, with a wide range of manufactured products. Philadelphia and New York were particularly important with a diversification of manufactures on the East Coast. Both cities were prominent in the garment industry and in retail merchandising. The third major manufacturing center was Cincinnati, Ohio, known in those days as

"Porkopolis" because of its expertise in what Charles Morris has called "disassembly lines," in which hogs were slaughtered and sliced down, "selling all but the squeal." A major industrial enterprise, Procter & Gamble, would emerge in that city, becoming a leading manufacturer of soap products initially made out of pork renderings.

The Midwest was also home to Cleveland, which became a center of oil refining, and served as the headquarters of the Standard Oil Company until 1885. Further west was Chicago, which became a diversified manufacturing center in such industries as meat packing and iron and steel production, as well as the headquarters of the McCormick enterprise, known for its agricultural reapers. Chicago also became a center of consumer merchandising, with Sears Roebuck and Montgomery Ward both located in that city.

Manufacturing also increased in the South, although the area continued to lag behind the rest of the country economically. Tobacco processing, iron and steel production, and textile manufacturing were the dominant areas of growth in the South.

The Protective Tariff System: Fencing Out Foreign Competition

The growth of the industrial economy in the United States from the 1860s to the end of the nineteenth century and the emergence of these centers of industry can be traced in part to the reinstitution of the protective tariff system. This had been a key element of Alexander Hamilton's 1791 "Report on the Subject of

Manufactures," which supported the continuance of the system of tariffs to permit domestic companies to "undersell" foreign competitors. Hamilton's insights were included as a major part of Henry Clay's "American System," which similarly sought to insulate United States companies from competition, while also providing revenues to fund internal improvements.

Protective tariffs became an integral part of the Republican platform throughout the nineteenth century. As President Benjamin Harrison announced in his 1889 inaugural address: "I look hopefully to the continuance of our protective system and to the consequent development of manufacturing and mining enterprises in the states hitherto wholly given to agriculture as a potent influence in the perfect unification of our people."

The tariff system served its key purpose by protecting domestic producers from foreign competition. It was wildly successful in facilitating domestic economic development. By 1900, 97 percent of the manufactured goods purchased by American consumers came from domestic producers. Particularly critical was the insulation of domestic iron and steel producers from competition from their English and German competitors, permitting American corporations to become the worldwide leader in iron and steel by the turn of the century.

Internal Improvements: The Railroad Network

The emergence of centers of industry in the East and Midwest was also fueled by construction of a national transportation system through the efforts of both the federal and state governments in the last half of the nineteenth century. That the federal government should finance the development of internal improvements, including roads, canals, harbors, and later, railroads, was not a new concept. It was a fundamental premise of Henry Clay's "American System" in the first half of the nineteenth century. Clay's vision, which was shared by Abraham Lincoln from his early days in Illinois state government, was to unite an expanding country through a system of canals and roads which would enable manufacturers to ship their goods more easily within a larger and united domestic market.

While Clay's vision was not shared by the Jacksonian Democrats who governed in much of the period immediately before the Civil War, the Republican Party which governed thereafter made internal improvements a major priority by supporting the development of railroads, waterways, harbors, and roads. Thus, President Ulysses Grant, in his second inaugural address in 1873, supported the "construction of cheap routes of transit throughout the land, to the end that the products of all may find a market and leave a living remuneration to the producer." President James Garfield similarly announced in his 1881 inaugural address that "Our facilities for transportation should be promoted by the continued improvements of our harbors and great interior waterways and by the increase of our tonnage on the ocean."

Republican support for the development of internal improvements was most striking and most successful in the case of railroads. By 1883, there were a total of four transcontinental railroads, including a southern route running from New Orleans to San Francisco. By 1900, there were 190,000 miles of railroad track, doubling the mileage of 1880, and railroads were a major employer, counting some one million workers in their employ. As Alexander Keyssar has aptly observed, the system of railroads "nationalized the economy," and knitted the country together through a transportation network which permitted shipment of both agricultural products and manufactured goods throughout the country, East to West and North to South. Moreover, as Charles Morris has observed, railroads "enabled" the development or expansion of multiple industries, including meat packing, steel, petroleum, and even factory farms.

The railroads did not stop at the sides of the tracks, as the railroad developers went on to erect warehouses, grain elevators, and stockyards adjacent to the tracks to facilitate (while monopolizing) commerce and uniting the two coasts. Railroads became so powerful that they were able to literally stop time, catalyzing the imposition of standard time zones throughout the country in 1883, in order to facilitate uniform timetables for railroad traffic.

Railroads were very much a creature of government, both federal and state. They were funded in large part by governmental grants, both direct and indirect. The most significant contribution came in the form of land grants. Railroads received over 130 million net acres of land from the federal government. These were given in the form of alternate sections, in a checkerboard pattern, ten to twenty miles on both sides of the tracks. The Northern Pacific Railroad alone ultimately received 44 million acres in such federal grants. State governments supplied land grants to railroads approximating an additional 50 million acres. While railroads often retained the best lands for themselves for future development or speculation, they also sold significant portions to settlers.

A second form of assistance came in the form of direct subsidies to the railroads. These subsidies totaled over $350 million in the period from 1861 to 1890. Further subsidies came in the form of tax exemptions and loans granted by both federal and state governments.

Immigration: Securing a Workforce

For industry to grow, an expanded workforce was required. Much of this need was met through immigration, which was encouraged at both the federal and state levels. As a result of liberal immigration policies, a flood of immigrants came to America, many of whom were employed in manufacturing operations in the Eastern and Midwestern states. Some of these workers were skilled laborers who had learned a trade in their native Europe, and thus were helpful in facilitating the growth of American industries. One of many such examples was Thomas Kay, an English weaver who emigrated first to the Eastern United States where he worked in a number of textile mills. He then moved to Oregon and started his own woolen mill. His family later took over another woolen mill which had failed and turned it around to become what is now the iconic Pendleton Woolen Mills of Portland, Oregon.

Unskilled immigrant labor was also critically needed, and became a key factor in building out the expanding railroad network. Indeed, Irish and Chinese immigrants were the main laborers on railroad construction. The Chinese immigrants mainly moved into California, with some 300,000 relocating to that state between 1853 and 1882. Chinese immigrants accounted for nine percent of California's population in 1860, and 25 percent of the California workforce in the 1870s. In San Francisco, this figure rose to 30 percent, with the Chinese tending to work in factories or in work which required inexpensive labor. Eventually, as the railroads were completed and the economy worsened, public opinion turned violently against Chinese immigration, with exclusionary laws enacted at the federal and California state levels in the final two decades of the nineteenth century, culminating in the 1902 Chinese Exclusion Act at the federal level. This legislation effectively ended Chinese immigration into this country. Perhaps the most telling vignette of this rampant anti-Chinese prejudice comes from the famous photograph of the laying of the "Golden Spike" which marked the completion of the first transcontinental railroad. Before the picture was taken, all of the Chinese laborers were removed from camera range.

Technology: The American System of Mass Production

New technologies also fueled the growth of American industry after the Civil War, and served as an additional factor in knitting the United States together into one market system. While railroads provided a national transportation network, the invention of the telephone and telegraph sparked a communications revolution which enabled industrial enterprises to operate more efficiently and rapidly. Railroad operations were similarly assisted by inventions, including more efficient and reliable steam engines and motors to drive the equipment; the air brake; the safety or auto coupler; and refrigerated freight cars, which permitted the safe and hygienic transportation of cattle meat to distant locations. Railroad traffic was also made more efficient by replacing wooden and iron rails with more stable steel, which came into wider use with the invention of new methods of processing. The key advance was the Bessemer Process, patented in 1855, which enabled steel to be mass produced at a significantly lower cost. Eleven steel mills employing the process were built in the United States between 1866 and 1877, and railroads were using steel rails on 93 percent of the domestic track mileage by 1900.

Beyond these specific inventions, there emerged a national industrial commitment to mass production and mass distribution. This was epitomized by the precision manufacture of guns with interchangeable parts by the Colt Patent Firearms Manufacturing Company, and became known as the American System of manufacture or the "push for scale." By perfecting uniformity and interchangeability of parts, industrial operations were enabled to expand both production and distribution efficiently.

Industry in The South

The South was recovering from the great losses of

the Civil War, both human and economic, during the Reconstruction period, and in the later years following 1877. While the South continued to lag behind the North and West in its economic development, there nevertheless was significant growth in several areas. Railroads, which had been destroyed by the Union Army during the Civil War, were rebuilt with track mileage doubling between 1880 and 1890. Southern industry also developed in three major areas. First, textile factories became common in several areas of the South. Second, James Duke dominated tobacco processing in North Carolina, building the American Tobacco Company into a powerful national monopoly. This tobacco industry, as well as cotton farmers, benefitted from newly developed commercial phosphate fertilizers. Third, and perhaps most significantly, a major iron and steel production capacity was developed in Birmingham, Alabama. By 1890, the South possessed approximately 20 percent of the total domestic capacity for iron and steel production.

Development of the West

While industry grew in the East, the Midwest, and even the South, much of the territory of the United States west of the Mississippi lay undeveloped as the Civil War ended. To create the national market envisioned by Henry Clay, it was necessary to open these vast tracts of land to swift development to construct a national market which stretched "from sea to shining sea." The Great Plains area, ranging from Montana and North Dakota in the North to Texas in the South, posed a particular challenge. It included approximately 20 percent of the continental United States land mass. Known as the "Great American Desert," the Great Plains posed multiple significant obstacles to its development. A second area requiring further development was the Far West land beyond the Rocky Mountains, which also required development and integration into an expanding United States economy and culture.

While the construction of the railroad network, and particularly the transcontinental railroad system and its subsidiary routes, provided the transportation facilities to develop the West, several other issues impeded Western development, particularly in the Great Plains. These included: a paucity of American settlers; the presence of both Native Americans and of great herds of buffalo on the Great Plains; and inadequate farming technology for development of a productive agriculture in the region. By addressing each of these issues, the United States was able to add eight new states between 1867 and 1890. These states were Nebraska, Colorado, North Dakota, South Dakota, Montana, Washington, Idaho, and Wyoming.

Homestead Laws

A sequence of federal homestead laws, sales of railroad land grant properties to prospective settlers, and liberal immigration laws each addressed the need to recruit people to populate the West. After the original Homestead Act of 1862, which we reviewed in the first chapter, three other legislative initiatives expanded the incentives for new settlers in the Great Plains and Far West. First came the Timber Culture Act of 1873, under which settlers could receive 160 acres of public land if they planted trees on 40 of those acres. Next came the Desert Land Act of 1877, which awarded 640 acres at a price of $1.25 an acre provided that the settler irrigated the land within three years. Finally, under the Timber and Stone Act of 1878, land suited for timber and stone development could be purchased at $2.50 an acre. Each measure sought to secure private development of public lands to expand the population west of the Mississippi. In turn, new settlers could ship agricultural and home goods back to the East or Midwest by railroad or water, and merchants from those parts of the country could in turn ship their manufactured and consumer goods to these settlers through this national transportation network of railroads, canals, and harbors.

The homestead laws were one factor which contributed to a major population spurt west of the Mississippi River from 1870 to 1890. The population more than doubled from 6,800,000 to 16,700,000 in this period, and approximately 500,000 acres of public lands were claimed by about 3 million settlers in Nebraska, Kansas, and the Dakotas. Only one-sixth of all public lands, however, were given to actual settlers, with the bulk going to speculators, many of whom were European absentee landlords who contracted with tenant farmers or others to develop the land for farming or ranching. Moreover, many actual settlers preferred to buy railroad lands, which were closer to shipping points, warehouses, and grain elevators, rather than to take the less desirable homestead lands.

Immigration

Immigration was another key factor in populating the Great Plains and Far West, as well as the East. From 1865 to 1890, for example, between 9 and 10 million immigrants relocated to the United States, providing both factory workers and farmer/settlers. The largest source of these settlers was immigration. In the Midwestern states of Minnesota, North Dakota, and Wisconsin foreign-born residents accounted for between 30 and 45 percent of the total population. Much of this relocation originated in the Scandinavian countries. Denmark lost one-third of its population through such emigration, and, calculated as a percentage of its population that emigrated, Norway was second only to Ireland in providing immigrants to America. The Scandinavian influence is recorded in many works of literature, including Willa Cather's *O Pioneers!* which relates the story of a Swedish immigrant family in Nebraska.

Native Americans

While homestead laws, railroad land, and liberal immigration laws were designed to populate the West, other efforts, both public and private, sought the opposite result of *depopulation*. The first and principal target of such efforts was the Native American with some 200,000 or more tribesmen who lived, hunted, and roamed over these lands. As popular "Cowboy and Indian" movies of the twentieth century such as John Ford's 1956 classic, "The Searchers," portrayed it, the Native Americans raided homesteads, killed the settlers in the most gruesome manners, and stole their children. These Native Americans also blocked new settlements and stopped railroad construction by attacks on the laborers clearing the land and laying the rails. The "Indians" therefore had to go; as the Union General and Civil War hero William Sherman put it, total war was waged against the Native American population, "even to their extermination" in the Indian Wars of the 1860s to 1890. In these wars, successive treaties struck by the federal government with multiple tribes fell like a line of dominos, ending with the massacre of at least 150 Native American men, women, and children by soldiers at Wounded Knee, South Dakota, on December 29, 1890. In California, "Indian hunting" became a sport and the Native American population in that state sunk from 150,000 in 1850 to 30,000 in 1880.

Most of the Native American population which survived the Indian wars was exiled to reservations. The Indian "problem" was now solved.

Buffalo

The second major effort at depopulation aimed to eliminate the buffalo, numbering over 15 million on the Great Plains as the Civil War ended in 1865. Vast herds of buffalo prevented settlement of many areas, stopped railroad construction, and slowed the development of the expanding cattle ranching industry. Thus, the buffalo also had to go. And they did. The 15 million buffalo of 1865 dwindled to 200,000 ten years later, a decrease of more than 98 percent. To achieve this bloody end, railroads hired trained hunters to kill them and also ran trains by buffalo lands with "sportsmen" shooting them from their seats.

Killing the buffalo also assisted Native American removal, since the tribes used every part of the buffalo for food, clothing, and other purposes down to the buffalo tendons, which were used as bow strings. Without the meat, the Native American would starve, and as another Union Civil War General, Philip Sheridan, pointed out, "starvation leads to surrender."

Technology

Development of the West was further assisted by the emergence of new inventions and technologies. Grants of patents doubled each year after the Civil War, with some 440,000 patents granted between 1860 and 1890. Given their importance to farming, and the difficulties presented by the harsh prairie lands of the Great Plains, 12,000 patents were granted on plows alone by 1900. One of the important early breakthroughs was the cast-steel plow perfected by John Deere, a Vermont native who relocated to Illinois in 1836, and whose eponymous company remains a worldwide industrial leader today. Deere's invention became famous as "The Plow that Broke the Plains."

Other inventions poured forth after the Civil War to assist the farmer and rancher. These included the self-binding reaper and header, Westinghouse threshers, planters and wire binders, and phosphate fertilizers. But the key invention which enabled the West to be farmed and to support cattle ranching was barbed wire, invented by J.F. Glidden in 1874. Barbed wire solved two major problems. First, it permitted cattle ranchers to secure their cattle safely inside defined boundaries. Second, the invention permitted farmers to protect their crops from cattle and other animals by fencing them within secure areas. The invention of barbed wire also solved the problem of the scarcity of lumber in the Great Plains which made wooden fences too expensive to construct in that region.

The Emerging Western Economy

Each of the factors listed above permitted settlement and development of the West. By 1900, agricultural and mining operations were important components of the Western economy. Farmers, cattle ranchers, and miners populated the West. While there were many small farmers, the popular literature extolling "the Little House on the Prairie" provides a skewed view of reality. Given the large absentee ownership of homestead lands, 25 percent of the farmland was operated by tenant farmers as part of large commercial farms which have grown today to dominate all domestic agricultural operations. The Midwest became "America's Breadbasket" providing the bulk of such staples as wheat, corn, and soy beans, with wheat being the dominant crop throughout the West.

Cattle ranching also became a major component of the Western economy. The Cattle Kingdom gave rise to "cow towns" such as Abilene, Kansas, and cattle were regularly driven on the Santa Fe Trail from Texas and the Midwest to Western destinations, or shipped by refrigerated rail cars for Eastern consumption.

Mining in the West was an additional key to the growth of the West in the period from the 1860s to the 1890s. Gold, silver, and copper were the principal elements for Western mining. While gold is associated most commonly with the earlier California Gold Rush, the largest supply of gold was actually found in Colorado, which mined over $1.2 billion worth of gold in the period from 1860 to 1890. Nevada, with the famous Comstock Lode, produced over $900 million worth of silver in the same period. Finally, Montana, with the Anaconda Copper Mines, led in the development of that mineral. Mineral mining of this nature also produced employment for hundreds of thousands of laborers, further helping to populate the West.

CHAPTER THREE
THE ADVENT OF REGULATION:
THE PRODUCERS STRIKE BACK

The pro-business initiatives of the Republican administrations in the last third of the nineteenth century were not embraced by the whole nation. Most prominent in the opposition were farmers in the Plains States, the Midwest, and the South. These self-styled "producers" organized in Farmers' Alliances, and were supported by some elements of the labor movement, particularly by railroad workers and miners. Each of these parties viewed themselves as victims of industrial capitalism and the monopolies they saw it as spawning. In response, they called for equal rights for all, without special privileges granted to any.

The Plight of the Farmers

Mary Elizabeth Lease of Kansas, one of the farmers' most vocal spokespersons, saw their problem as "Wall Street owns the country... The West and South are bound and prostrate before the manufacturing East."

Lease urged the farmers to raise "less corn and more hell" to remedy their plight.

In the last quarter of the nineteenth century, the farming population experienced a number of significant problems rooted in economic turmoil, a limited money supply, harsh credit terms, and monopoly pricing by the trusts of the period. To begin with, an economic downturn depressed the market prices of crops such as cotton, corn, and wheat more than 50 percent from 1881 to 1894. In some parts of the West and South, it actually cost farmers more to raise their crops than the prices at which they could sell them. Moreover, because of the "sound money" or deflationary policies pursued by the Republican administrations, farmers who had borrowed in inflated dollars had to pay back their loans in deflated dollars, resulting in a situation where in real terms it took double the number of bushels of wheat, corn, and other crops to repay a debt in 1887 than it did in 1867. All of this was compounded by a serious drought in 1889 and 1890 in the Midwest. These economic problems led to widespread foreclosures on farmlands when farmers were unable to keep their mortgage payments current. In Kansas alone, some 43 percent of all homes were lost to bank foreclosures.

Even farmers who avoided foreclosure continued to be burdened by the high interest rates charged by banks and other lenders. New technology which created expensive labor-saving devices such as the cast-steel plow and the self-binding reaper was financed at interest rates ranging between 18 and 36 percent. Farmers also saw themselves as victimized by the protective tariff policies of the Republicans, since those policies effectively foreclosed foreign competition which might have supplied products needed by the farmers at lower prices. A different type of credit problem affected farmers in the South. In that region, there were few banks and farmers often obtained the goods they needed from local "country stores" which utilized the crop-lien system. That system required the farmer to collateralize his loan with crops mandated by the country store. This led to the "no cotton, no credit" approach complained of by southern farmers.

Farmers also fell prey to railroad monopolies. As N.B. Ashby of the Northern Farmers' Alliance put it, railroads were the "prolific parent of the trust, the trade combine, and trade conspiracy." The railroad was, as the novelist Frank Norris wrote, an "Octopus," controlling not only shipping on the rails, but also storage of grain in facilities it owned at rail side. This monopoly power was exercised in a discriminatory fashion in favor of large corporations, at the expense of the small farmer. Farmers were charged higher rates for shipping their goods than corporations were, and railroads charged corporations less for long hauls than farmers were charged for short hauls. In addition, railroads were often the mortgagees on the farmland they sold to new settlers at inflated prices.

The Farmers' Response

In response to the multiple problems which they faced, farmers organized. There were two particularly important groups which were formed after the Civil

War. The first group, The Patrons of Husbandry, which was popularly known as the Grange, was formed in 1867 and grew to a membership of more than 850,000 in 1875. It had early legislative successes in four Midwest states (Iowa, Illinois, Minnesota, and Wisconsin) which passed "Granger laws" regulating rates charged by railroads and grain elevators.

A second group of Farmers' Alliances was an even more significant force in the time period from 1877 through the 1890s. Organized by separate regions, and separated into Caucasian and African-American alliances in the South, these groups reached a membership of approximately 4,000,000 in the South and Midwest. The Farmers' Alliances were heavily Protestant and emphasized farmer education through Alliance newspapers, lending libraries, camp meetings, religious services, fraternal organizations, and "traveling lecturers" who came and spoke to these farmers' groups to educate them on the business of farming. Women such as Mary Elizabeth Lease were a major part of these quasi-evangelical Alliances. The Alliances also taught farmers "Producer History" to balance what they referred to as the "Whig History" which celebrated industry and capital.

The Condition of Labor

The intellectual leadership of the Farmers' Alliances also saw the laborers of the country as co-producers, and attempted to recruit them into their movement against monopoly and capital. Labor was equally suffering in the last quarter of the nineteenth century. Wealthy monopolists, railroads, and large corporations were reducing wages and worsening working conditions. This led to several notable and often violent labor strikes from 1877 through 1894. In the Great Railroad Strike of 1877, railroad workers reacted to a 10 percent across-the-board reduction in their wages by calling a violent strike which began in West Virginia and ultimately spread across the country, reaching San Francisco. While it only lasted two weeks, the national death toll reached 50 and railroads lost property and profits approximating $30 million. Federal troops and state militia were called out in both West Virginia and Pennsylvania to put down the workers. In Pittsburgh, Pennsylvania, alone, more than 2000 railroad cars of the Pennsylvania Railroad, along with 104 of its locomotives, were destroyed.

In 1886, workers called for a national general strike in favor of an eight-hour workday. Demonstrations were held across the country, and in Chicago police fired on the strikers in that city, killing several of them. After anarchists called a meeting to protest that police action, a bomb was thrown into a group of the protesters, killing seven policemen, and injuring 67 in the crowd. Eight anarchists were indicted for murder, and four were convicted and executed.

The next major strike was launched in 1892 against the Homestead, Pennsylvania, steel mill owned by Andrew Carnegie, and operated by Henry Frick. Frick had imposed pay cuts and refused to negotiate with the steelworkers' union. Expecting violence, Frick hired 300 private Pinkerton police, and his decision led to violent confrontations between the Pinkertons and the workers, which culminated in the deaths of at least 12 people and injuries sustained by many others. Pennsylvania's governor sent the 8000 man Pennsylvania state militia to maintain order in Homestead, and leading newspapers denounced what the *New York Times* referred to as the "mob rule" of the workers.

The final major strike of the nineteenth century took place in 1894 and involved the Pullman Company, which manufactured luxury railroad cars. This followed the Panic of 1893, which was the most significant depression in American history prior to the Great Depression of the 1930s. It resulted in widespread unemployment affecting 20 percent of all American workers. The Pullman Company reacted by cutting employee wages from 25 to 40 percent. When Eugene Debs' American Railway Union led a boycott of Pullman railroad cars, this strike disrupted national transportation and caused the Democratic President Grover Cleveland to call in federal troops and obtain a federal court injunction against the strikers. The injunction was ignored and 25 soldiers were killed, leading to the arrest of Debs, who was sentenced to six months in jail for contempt of the court injunction. This led Debs to become a socialist, and a perennial candidate for president beginning in 1900 and ending only in 1920.

Two unions sought to join forces with the Farmers' Alliances. In addition to Debs' American Railway Union, the Knights of Labor played an important role in the early history of the Alliances. Formed in 1869, the Knights had a membership of over 700,000 in 1885. The Knights were composed mainly of small producers and, unlike the American Federation of Labor which refused to join the Alliance movement, recruited both skilled and unskilled laborers, as well as both whites and blacks in the North and South. To take one example, thousands of coal miners from Pennsylvania in the North to several states in the South became members of the Knights. The only persons excluded from membership in the Knights were bankers, lawyers, gamblers, and alcoholics.

A final group of workers which cooperated with the Farmers' Alliances in what Charles Postel has called a "commonwealth of reform" was miners, particularly in the West. They were both underpaid and subjected to dangerous working conditions. As one mine owner put it, when refusing to purchase additional lumber to shore up the mine shafts, "men are cheaper than timbers." The willingness of the miners and Debs' railroad workers to work with the Alliances is explained in part by the proximity in the Plains States and in the West of railroad workers and miners to the farmers in those regions, and the recognition of the common problems which they experienced and which they attributed to the predation of the railroads and the monopolists.

Presidential Elections and Third Parties

Given the significant problems being experienced by the large population of farmers and workers at the time, resort to the ballot box was to be expected. Indeed, in the elections of 1880, 1884, and 1888, the percentage of the eligible electorate which voted ranged between approximately 75 percent and 82 percent. While turnout was high, the margins of victory in those elections were quite narrow: approximately 10,000 votes in 1880, 23,000 votes in 1884, and 100,000 votes in 1888, with the first two being decided by less than 2/10s of one percent of the vote. The third resulted in a victory only in the Electoral College by Benjamin Harrison, who lost the popular vote by 100,000.

Despite these large turnouts and close elections, neither the Republican nor the Democratic Party was responsive to the problems being experienced by the farmers and workers. Instead, both parties were sympathetic to the interests of business, with their only major difference being in the opposition of Democrats to protective tariffs, an opposition based in part on the close ties between some top Democrats and business leaders with great interests in foreign markets.

A striking illustration of the failure of both parties to protect the farmer came in President Grover Cleveland's veto of a bill which would have appropriated $50,000 to buy grain for farmers experiencing drought conditions. Moreover, Cleveland's Democratic administration also called in federal troops against the railway workers in the Pullman strike.

Under these circumstances, significant third parties emerged and secured votes which would have been sufficient to turn the close elections from 1880 through 1888. In 1880, for example, James B. Weaver, a former Union Army officer, secured 3.4 percent of the presidential vote as the candidate of the Greenback Party, which favored an inflated currency and a return to paper currency not backed by either gold or silver. In 1888, it was the Prohibition Party which secured 2.2 percent of the total presidential vote. As we will discuss below, however, it was not until the emergence of the Populist Party and the presidential election of 1892 that the third-party movement secured a significant vote.

Legislative Responses

Despite their failure to recruit either of the major parties to their agendas, the Grangers and the Farmers' Alliances were nevertheless able to secure passage of some regulatory legislation. On the state level in the Midwest, they were successful in the 1870s in obtaining the Granger Laws mentioned above. Those laws set maximum railroad and grain elevator rates, removing price-setting discretion from the owners, thereby threatening their profit margins. In other states, however, legislatures dominated by big business defeated attempts at increased regulation. To take just one example, Rockefeller interests were said to have done everything to the Pennsylvania legislature "except [to] refine it." And, in the same state, appointments of federal court judges were purportedly subject to a *de facto* veto by the Pennsylvania Railroad well into the twentieth century.

Other regulation was imposed at the federal level toward the end of the nineteenth century. Initially, the 1887 Interstate Commerce Commission Act established an administrative agency to protect farmers and others by capping railroad rates at levels deemed by the ICC to be "just and reasonable." The Act further banned railroads from charging rates which the agency saw as discriminatory; from granting rebates; and from charging different rates for long-haul and short-haul traffic. These practices raised railroad profits, but discriminated against farmers and other small producers in favor of large corporations and trusts. While this Act proved to be largely ineffective, it did represent a start in regulating the railroads at the federal level.

The ICC Act was followed in 1890 by enactment of the Sherman Antitrust Act in response to the emergence of "Trusts" which had monopolized many key industries. The Trust device, which was invented by Standard Oil in 1882, permitted the voting stock of separate corporations to be turned over to common trustees who administered all of the ostensibly separate corporate operations. The Trust mechanism thereby concentrated corporate power in the dominant trusts, reducing competition and fostering monopoly. Indeed, by 1900, the Trust device had become so popular and widespread that what had been over 5000 corporations was effectively reduced to about 300 through the utilization of this corporate device.

In response to these developments, the Sherman Act sought to restore competition in several ways. First, the statute declared illegal, without any exceptions, "[e]very contract, combination in the form of trust or otherwise, or conspiracy" which restrained trade or commerce, and declared any person who made such a contract, or engaged in any such combination or conspiracy, guilty of a misdemeanor. Second, in similarly broad language, any person who engaged in actual or attempted monopolization, or in a combination or conspiracy with another to monopolize any part of interstate or international trade or commerce, was likewise deemed guilty of a misdemeanor. Criminal fines and/or imprisonment "not exceeding one year" were mandated for violations of any of these provisions, and the United States Attorneys in every district were placed under a "duty" to initiate lawsuits to "prevent and restrain" violations. On their face, these broad proscriptions to be enforced criminally as well as civilly, appeared to erect formidable barriers to corporate concentration, price-fixing, and other anti-competitive practices. As we will see below, however, the courts radically restricted the scope of the Sherman Act prohibitions.

The Emergence of the Populist Party

The most serious third-party challenge to the pro-business policies of both the Republican and Democratic Parties came from the Populist Party, which had its greatest influence in the period from 1889 to 1896. In the mid-1890s, the Populist Party secured between 25 and 45 percent of the total vote in some 20-odd states and elected as many as six United States senators. Its 1892 presidential candidate, the same James Weaver who had run as the Greenback Party candidate in 1880, polled 1 million votes, representing 8.5 percent of the total presidential vote. He secured 22 electoral votes, winning a majority of the total popular vote in the states of Kansas, Colorado, Nevada, and Idaho.

The Populists were a colorful coalition of many groups, including farmers' alliances, labor unions, women's organizations, and what Charles Postel has described as "an array of nonconformists, including urban radicals, tax and currency reformers, prohibitionists, middle-class utopians, spiritual innovators, and miscellaneous iconoclasts." Populist thinkers provided a powerful fact-based critique of the major parties' pro-business policies, all based on the perception that monopoly power deprived the common producer of the equal rights owed to all. Here are some of the Populist voices:

S.O. Daws, a traveling lecturer for the Texas Alliance, told his farmer audience that its members had an "obligation to stand as a great conservative body against the encroachments of monopolies and in opposition to the growing corruption of wealth and power."

Populist Governor Lorenzo Lewelling of Kansas proclaimed that government must "protect the producer from the ravages of combined wealth."

L.L. Polk, a major Populist leader and a former Confederate soldier from North Carolina, announced that "You will see arrayed on the one side the great magnates of the country, and Wall Street brokers, and the plutocratic power; and on the other you will see the people."

"Sockless" Jerry Simpson, a Kansas senator, summed up the Populist crusade as "a struggle between the robbers and the robbed."

The Populist Platform

Believing that capitalism was not a self-regulating system, the Populist Party called upon government to rein in capitalism's excesses, either through government ownership or by strict regulation. In order to deliver the producer from the maw of monopoly, Populist thinkers focused on what Norman Pollack has described as "the well-known trinity of land, transportation and money."

Land. In protest against the large grants of public lands made by Republican administrations to the railroads, and in further protest against the sale of public lands to foreign owners, the 1892 Omaha Platform of the Populist Party called for "reclaim[ing]" such land grants in whole or in part. Reasoning that "The land, including all the natural sources of wealth, is the heritage of the people, and should not be monopolized for speculative purposes," the Platform demanded that "alien ownership of land should be prohibited. All land now held by railroads and other corporations in excess of their actual needs, and all lands now owned by aliens, should be reclaimed by the government and held for actual settlers only."

The prohibition sought against alien ownership of land was rooted in the experience of dealing with absentee owners in the West who often foreclosed access by "actual settlers" to water and transportation. In Colorado, for example, absentee British landowners owned much of the irrigation system.

Transportation. In the area of transportation, the 1892 Populist Platform called for public ownership of the railroads. It proclaimed that "the time has come when the railroad corporations will either own the people or the people must own the railroads." It therefore supported the proposition that "the government should own and operate the railroads in the interest of the people" because transportation was "a means of exchange and a public necessity."

In a further attempt to rein in the power of the railroads and other large corporations, a Supplemental Resolution put the Populists on record as opposing "any subsidy or national aid to any private corporation for any purpose." While this resolution was never adopted on the federal level, many Western states and some others such as New Jersey included comparable provisions in their state constitutions.

Money. The money issue was the subject of multiple declarations in the Populist Platform. It called for a national currency which was "safe, sound, and flexible;" "free and unlimited coinage of silver and gold at the present legal ratio of sixteen to one;" and increasing of "the amount of circulating medium... to not less than fifty dollars per capita." As Robert McMath has aptly observed, the financial planks were "a recapitulation of greenbackism," a reference to paper dollars, which represented a debtor-friendly inflated currency, and had previously been utilized during he Civil War.

Another part of the Platform supported the Farmers' Alliance concept of a sub-treasury, which was refined into a sophisticated plan by Farmers' Alliance leader Charles W. Macune of Texas. The Sub-Treasury Plan called upon the government to construct and operate federal warehouses into which farmers could deposit their crops. Farmers would in turn receive negotiable certificates from the government which would trade as "full legal tender for all debts, public and private." The farmer would receive a loan from the government in an amount representing 80 percent of the crop value at an interest rate of only one percent. The Plan would deliver the farmers from the mercy of railroad- or otherwise-owned storage facilities, and provide working capital directly to the farmers, rescuing them from the national banks, which charged much higher interest rates. While Macune's Plan was widely ridiculed by business interests and the national press, it provided a clever and useful mechanism for farmers to finance their operations and their lives at a much lower cost. A variant of the Sub-Treasury Plan was ultimately incorporated in the Warehouse Act of 1916, under which the federal Department of Agriculture licensed warehouses which could store crops.

As these provisions demonstrate, Populists were in favor of a range of monetary reforms going well beyond utilizing silver as an additional metallic standard for the dollar. After 1892, however, the silver interests and some Democrats made it the key component of a fused Democrat-Populist Platform of 1896. Silver was seen as the key for increasing the currency, and bimetallism became popularized in the enormously successful 1894 publication, *Coins Financial School*. Written by William H. ("Coin") Harvey, this illustrated book sold hundreds of thousands of copies. Featuring "Professor Coin," the book was packed with facts and figures on the history of silver and gold, with the good professor rebutting every attack from those in the audience favoring the gold standard, which had the support of both the Republican and Democratic Parties at the time. Coin's recitation of facts and figures was followed by acid-laced attacks on the trusts and foreign moneylenders. Coin proclaimed that "A financial trust has control of your money, and with it, is robbing you of your property. Vampires feed upon your commercial blood." In his lectures, he contended that British interests used gold to keep the United States economy depressed, and that bringing back silver would not only help the debtors of this country, but would also invigorate and expand the domestic economy. The book drew upon the significant popular support for an easy fix to the problems caused to the farming community by tight money policies. Support for an expansion of the money supply went back to the early days of the Republic, long before the Greenback Party led by General Weaver raised it again in the 1880 presidential campaign.

Banks. While not expressly addressed in the Populist Platform, the power of banks was a major concern, especially to the farmer base of the Party who often lost their homes through mortgage foreclosures undertaken by the bankers. Mary Elizabeth Lease spoke forcefully against the power of the national banks. In the 160 speeches she made for the Populists in 1890, an important part of her message called for direct borrowing from the government on mortgages: "We want the abolition of the National Banks, and we want the power to make loans direct from the government. We want the accursed foreclosure system wiped out."

Corporations and Business. Populists had a particular suspicion of, and dislike for, the modern industrial corporation. In General Weaver's view, "through evolution in crime the corporation has taken the place of the pirate." A Populist newspaper in Nebraska echoed the same view in an 1896 article which characterized corporations as "great engines of oppression" which "lift up the rich and crush down the poor." The 1892 Populist Platform addressed this issue both in its Preamble, and in its second Declaration. The Preamble, composed by Ignatius Donnelly of Minnesota, whom John D. Hicks considered "perhaps the greatest orator of Populism," proclaimed that "The fruits of the toil of millions are boldly stolen to build up colossal fortunes for a few, unprecedented in the history of mankind; and the possessors of these, in turn, despise the republic and endanger liberty." The second Declaration in the Platform contained a similar theme, stating that "Wealth belongs to him who creates it, and every dollar taken from industry without an equivalent is robbery... The interests of rural and civic labor are the same; their enemies are identical." As noted above, moreover, the Platform opposed any type of subsidy or aid to any private corporation for any purpose.

Immigration. In opposition to the liberal immigration policies pursued by Republican administrations, the Populists "demand[ed] the further restriction of undesirable immigration," because "the present system... opens our ports to the pauper and criminal classes of the world, and crowds out our wage-earners."

Technology. The Populists also called for the government to own and operate the telegraph and telephone systems since these technological inventions, "like the post-office system," were "a necessity for the transmission of news." Many Populists would have gone further than nationalizing only the telegraph and telephone. As one Populist newspaper put it in 1895, "Government ownership of the great monopolies is our main idea."

Other Measures. In a further attempt to combat the combined wealth and power of rich industrialists such as John D. Rockefeller of Standard Oil and steel magnate Andrew Carnegie, several additional declarations and supplemental resolutions were adopted at the Populist Party's 1892 Convention. These called for, among other things, "That the union of the labor forces of the United States this day consummated shall be permanent and perpetual;" abolition of the use of "mercenaries" and "hired assassins of plutocracy" such as the private Pinkerton police engaged by Henry Frick in the Homestead Steel strike; term limits on the offices of President and Vice President, limiting both to one term only; direct election of United States senators by the people; and a graduated income tax. Before the Populist Party fused with the Democrats in 1896, it was successful only on one of these proposals. An income tax was imposed by Congress in 1894 in the amount of two percent on all incomes in excess of $4000. Even that success, however, was short-lived, since the Supreme Court of United States struck the tax down as unconstitutional.

Business Goes to Court

In an effort to forestall the legislative initiatives of the Grangers, the Farmers' Alliances, and the Populists, business interests sued to have some of the regulatory laws sponsored by these groups declared unconstitutional. This led Populist leaders in the 1890s to denounce the courts. Governor Lorenzo Lewelling of Kansas claimed that "the Courts and Judges of this country have become the mere tools and vassals and jumping-jacks of the great corporations that pull the string while the courts and judges dance." General Weaver agreed, arguing that "a bold and aggressive plutocracy...has not hesitated to tamper with our Court of last resort."

At first, the courts were friendly to the reforms. In the *Granger Cases* (1877), the Supreme Court of the United States upheld several of these regulatory laws. As Chief Justice Morrison Waite concluded in his majority opinion in *Munn v. Illinois* (1877), an Illinois law fixing maximum rates for grain storage warehouses in Chicago was constitutional because those warehouses affected the public interest. As such, "when...one devotes his property to a use in which the public has an interest, he, in effect, grants to the public an interest in that use, and must submit to be controlled by the public for the common good, to the extent of the interest he has thus created." Moreover, he saw the law in question as one designed to meet "this new development of commercial progress."

While the *Granger Cases* seemed promising to the reformers, a dissenting opinion by Justice Stephen J. Field was more accurate in charting the future approach the Supreme Court would be taking when analyzing regulatory legislation affecting business operations. Field saw the warehouse legislation as "subversive of the rights of private property," and argued that the majority's suggestion that business could only obtain relief from regulation from the legislature which enacted the restrictions in question meant that "all property and all business in the State are held at the mercy of a majority of its legislature."

Less than a decade after the *Granger Cases*, and in the context of labor violence, the Supreme Court shifted its attitude towards legislation which regulated business operations. To begin with, in *County of Santa Clara v. Southern Pacific R.R. Co.* (1886), Chief Justice Waite announced, without hearing argument on the question, that all of the members of the court were of the opinion that "the provision in the Fourteenth Amendment..., which forbids a state to deny to any person within its jurisdiction the equal protection of the laws, applies to these [railroad] corporations." Next, in *Wabash, St. Louis & Pacific Ry. Co. v. Illinois* (1886), the court ruled that the Interstate Commerce Clause barred states from regulating rates charged by railroads for the intrastate portion of a longer interstate trip. Even where states were permitted to regulate railroad rates in a case of traffic which was confined within state boundaries, the court ruled that such regulation must comply with the Fourteenth Amendment's due process requirement. Thus, in *Chicago, Milwaukee & St. Paul Ry. Co. v. Minnesota* (1890), the court struck down as unconstitutional a state statute which made rates set by a state commission final and not subject to judicial review. The court ruled that the statute "deprives the company of its rights to a judicial investigation, by due process of law, under the forms and with the machinery provided by the wisdom of successive ages for the investigation judicially of the truth of a matter in controversy, and substitutes therefor, as an absolute finality, the action of the railroad commission which, in view of the powers conceded to it by the state court, cannot be regarded as clothed with judicial functions, or possessing the machinery of a court of justice." Three dissenting judges saw this ruling as one which "practically overrules *Munn v. Illinois*... and the several railroad cases that were decided at the same time."

The court extended these rulings even further in the last decade of the nineteenth century. For example, in *Smyth v. Ames* (1898), the court ruled that since railroads were "persons" within the meaning of that term in the Fourteenth Amendment, their economic rights were protected against actions taken by a Nebraska state transportation board which set rates causing the railroads to operate at a loss. In his opinion for a unanimous court, Justice John Marshall Harlan declared that "the duty rests upon all courts, federal and state, when their jurisdiction is properly invoked, to see to it that no right secured by the supreme law of the land is impaired or destroyed by legislation. This function and duty of the judiciary distinguishes the American system from all other systems of government. The perpetuity of our institutions, and the liberty which is enjoyed under them, depend, in no small degree, upon the power given the judiciary to declare null and void all legislation that is clearly repugnant to the supreme law of the land." That the court was becoming resistant to the reform efforts sponsored by the Populists was perhaps most tellingly illustrated by the fact that Nebraska's argument to uphold its regulatory authority was presented to the

Supreme Court by the defeated Democratic-Populist 1896 presidential candidate, William Jennings Bryan, who lost again, this time in the courts.

During the same time period, the Supreme Court also voiced its displeasure for the widespread labor violence discussed above. For example, *In Re Debs* (1895) unanimously upheld the conviction of Eugene Debs for contempt of court for ignoring an injunction against the Pullman strikers. Notably, the opinion of the court used the term "mob" four times, and emphasized that "under the government of and by the people the means of redress of all wrongs are through the courts and at the ballot box, and that no wrong, real or fancied, carries with it legal warrant to invite as a means of redress the cooperation of a mob, with its accompanying acts of violence." A further reference by the Supreme Court to disapproval of labor violence appears in the separate opinion of Justice Stephen Field in *Pollock v. Farmers Loan & Trust Co.* (1895), the case which struck down the two percent federal income tax on incomes over $4000. Field warned that "the present assault on capital is but the beginning. It will be but the stepping-stone to others, larger and more sweeping, till our political contests will become a war of the poor against the rich, a war constantly growing in intensity and bitterness."

The court continued its pro-business rulings in some of its early decisions interpreting the reach of the Sherman Antitrust Act. In the first major antitrust case coming before it, the Supreme Court ruled in *Knight Co. v. United States* (1895), that the acquisition of four local sugar companies by the American Sugar Refining Company did not violate the antitrust laws, even though the combination resulted in the acquiring company controlling over 98 percent of the domestic market in refined sugar. This was because the antitrust laws could only constitutionally apply to "commerce," and could not extend to "manufacture." Chief Justice Melville Fuller's opinion explained that "Commerce succeeds to manufacture, and is not part of it. The power to regulate commerce is the power to prescribe the rule by which commerce shall be governed, and is a power independent of the power to suppress monopoly."

By extending the protections of the Fourteenth Amendment to railroads and other corporations, by denouncing and upholding punishments for labor violence, by striking down an income tax, and by narrowly construing the reach of the Sherman Act, the Supreme Court proved to be a relief valve for corporations and business owners as the nineteenth century ended. The reformers' legislative accomplishments were thus threatened, and sometimes reversed, on the steps of the highest court in the land.

The Death of the Populist Party

While the Populists increased their total vote in the 1894 congressional and state elections from their 1892 presidential tally of 1,000,000 votes to nearly 1,500,000 votes, and the Party gained both congressional and state offices in 1894, it became clear to many of the Populist leaders that joining with one of the major political parties was the only mechanism which would permit them to attain sufficient political power to implement their agenda. At the presidential level, this led to fusion with the Democratic Party, and a majority of Populists endorsed the Democratic nominee, William Jennings Bryan, as their candidate in 1896. Silver became the principal uniting factor, since it was seen as a vehicle to increase the money supply, aiding farmers and debtors generally by permitting repayment of their debts in a inflated, and therefore, cheaper currency, thereby implementing the views of the imaginary Professor Coin. As a result of this focus on adding silver to back the currency and replacing the gold (only) standard with what became known as bimetallism, much of the remaining Populist Platform fell by the wayside. As Populist leader and muckraking journalist Henry Demarest Lloyd put it, "Free silver is the cow-bird of the reform movement. It waited until the nest had been built by the sacrifices and labors of others, and then laid its own eggs in it, pushing out the others which lay smashed on the ground."

Bryan lost the election to the Republican candidate, William McKinley, by about 600,000 votes, in a vigorously contested election where the turnout exceeded 79 percent of the eligible voters. McKinley won the electoral vote 271 to 176, winning the Northeast and the upper Midwest. Bryan took the West and South, and a difference of less than 20,000 votes in six other states would have given him the presidency.

Why did the Democrat/Populists lose? While, as William Allen White put it, Bryan "unashamedly made his cause that of the poor and oppressed," he came across as an Evangelical Christian on a quasi-religious crusade, and his message therefore failed to resonate with either Catholics or the more established Protestant denominations. In addition, business was able to beat back the largest challenge to its agenda since the Civil War by enlisting the mainstream media, academics, religious and other opinion leaders on its side, and by threatening bankruptcies, factory shutdowns, and job losses if Bryan and his "anarchists" were elected and protective tariffs were eliminated or significantly reduced. McKinley, moreover, was able to appeal to both Catholics and German Lutherans, significantly raising the votes of these groups for him 15 to 20 percent over the presidential votes they cast for the Republican candidate in 1892. Part of this success can be attributed to the Republican distribution of thousands of political pamphlets written in nine separate languages, and McKinley's long-term support for both labor and for Catholics, support which earned him the opposition of the nativist American Protective Association, and the support or lack of opposition from some labor unions. Indeed, John Ireland, the Catholic Archbishop of St. Paul, Minnesota, visibly supported McKinley against Bryan. Finally, McKinley was seen as the candidate of prosperity, fiscal responsibility, economic stability, sound money, national markets, and patriotism. By contrast, even his admirer, the poet Vachel Lindsay, saw Bryan as divisive, "Smashing Plymouth Rock with his boulders from the West." And Bryan failed utterly in the East; failed with all of labor, except Eugene Debs' railway workers and some mining organizations; and failed with non-evangelical Christians. The producers' crusade foundered as the nineteenth century came to an end, while industry prospered.

CHAPTER FOUR
THE SECOND ROUND OF REGULATION:
THE PROGRESSIVE MOVEMENT

The Decline and Fall of the Populist Party and the Emergence of the Progressive Movement

By 1900, the Populist Party was effectively absorbed into the Democratic Party, and was little more than a memory. A faithful Populist remnant nominated Wharton Barker, a Philadelphia investment banker, as its presidential candidate in 1900, but Barker received only 50,000 votes. This was less than one quarter of the vote of the Prohibition Party candidate.

The task of reforming the nation's existing economic and social system was taken up by a different mix of reformers who became known as "Progressives." The Progressive Movement was an amorphous mix of several different strands of reformers. As such, it lacked the cohesion provided by the Farmers' Alliances for the Populists. Moreover, while the Populists were mainly agrarian, the Progressives were generally members of an urban elite which Theodore Roosevelt referred to as "the best people." Progressives were mainly Protestants who viewed themselves as natural moral leaders. Their overriding vision was to impose structure and order on an increasingly diverse society in order to "reconstruct" it socially, economically, politically, and spiritually. Their urban-oriented reforms differed as such from those favored by the mainly agrarian Populists.

Progressives opposed the prevailing nineteenth-century laissez-faire philosophy, calling instead for a more active government which would shape American society and protect and transform the poor, immigrants, women, and children into a new American community of responsible citizens. In politics, this meant regaining control of urban governments from political leaders who were supported by large immigrant communities.

The leaders of this new Progressive movement possessed what Theodore Roosevelt described as "a fierce discontent with evil." As such, they approached their work with a moral certitude that they were right in directing their efforts to eradicate "sins against society." In economics, Progressives echoed the Populists in seeking to abolish or control monopoly, as well as to redistribute wealth through a federal income tax, which ultimately was ratified in 1913 in the Sixteenth Amendment. But Progressives also had what to them was the higher purpose of constructing a new society with what the Protestant cleric Washington Gladden described as "a different kind of men and women."

In politics, Progressives saw an emerging conflict, in the words of journalist Ray Stannard Baker of

McClure's Magazine, "between two great parties, one a progressive party seeking to give the government more power in business affairs, the other a conservative party striving to retain all the power possible in private hands. One looks towards socialism, the other obstinately defends individualism."

The diverse group of Progressives can be divided into five principal elements. These are journalists and novelists; management experts; women's groups; religious reformers; and politicians. The first group, which Theodore Roosevelt christened as "muckrakers," was catalyzed by the highly influential *McClure's Magazine*. Founded by S.S. McClure in 1893, the magazine devoted much of its efforts to exposing illegal acts of the great monopolies, and political corruption at the local, state, and national levels. *McClure's* had a collection of impressive staff writers, including Ida Tarbell, Ray Stannard Baker, and Lincoln Steffens. Tarbell, for example, wrote some 24 articles exposing the predatory practices of the Standard Oil Company, and those articles were republished as a two-volume book, *A History of the Standard Oil Company*, in 1904. The articles and book were influential in persuading the federal government to file a successful antitrust suit to break up Standard Oil. In politics, a series of articles by Lincoln Steffens which also found their way into a book, *The Shame of the Cities*, exposed municipal corruption across the country in cities including St. Louis and Philadelphia.

S. S. McClure also financed independent novelists including Upton Sinclair, whose exposé of the meat packing industry, *The Jungle* (1906), led to federal legislation regulating meat packing, and Frank Norris, whose novel, *The Octopus* (1901), documented in a fictional mode the predatory practices of the Southern Pacific Railroad directed against farmers in California. Norris' work was instrumental in securing the passage of federal legislation regulating railroad practices in 1903 and 1906.

McClure's became a significant political force assisting the reform efforts of Theodore Roosevelt's presidency, but its influence waned after its high-powered staff writers left to form their own magazine in 1906.

Other magazines followed *McClure's* muckraking efforts. *The Cosmopolitan* magazine, owned by William Randolph Hearst, for example, ran a nine-part series in 1906 by David Graham Phillips entitled "The Treason of the Senate." Phillips' work documented the ties of certain United States Senators to big business, and was the immediate precipitating cause of Theodore Roosevelt's famous "muckraking" comment.

A second major strand of Progressives was composed of management experts of several types. This was the era of scientific management pioneered by Frederick Winslow Taylor. Taylor popularized the concept of time management, which was implemented most prominently in the famous assembly line of the Ford Motor Company. Reliance upon experts also characterized several notable municipal reform movements, including the installation of professional city managers and the formation of municipal research bureaus which fought political corruption and addressed environmental issues such as the great floods which ravaged Galveston, Texas, in 1900, and Dayton, Ohio, in 1913.

Business, medicine, law, and education also became more organized along professional lines. In business, national associations emerged, including the National Association of Manufacturers (1895), and the United States Chamber of Commerce (1912). In medicine, the American Medical Association (1901) inaugurated scientific admissions standards, while state bar associations imposed licensing standards upon would-be lawyers. Finally, in education, major universities instituted tenure systems under which only Ph.D.s would be eligible for advancement and permanent positions.

Progressives also included a number of women's groups. Indeed, some historians date the beginning of the Progressive Movement to the 1889 opening of Hull House in Chicago, a settlement house begun by Jane Addams to educate immigrants. Four hundred such settlement houses were started over the country by the early 1900s. A second element in the women's reform movements included women's clubs, which lobbied for political reform and women's suffrage. The latter crusade was instrumental in securing the ratification of the Nineteenth Amendment in 1920, which provided that the right of citizens to vote "shall not be denied or abridged by the United States or by any State on account of sex."

The final major organization in the women's reform movement was the Women's Christian Temperance Union of Frances Willard, which had 200,000 members by 1898, and supported women's suffrage, equal pay for women, and prohibition. The efforts of the WCTU were instrumental in securing the ratification of the Eighteenth Amendment, imposing prohibition, in 1919.

A fourth influential segment of the over-all Progressive Movement was the Social Gospel Movement of Protestant ministers who focused on bringing "the Kingdom of God to earth." These reformers popularized the saying "What Would Jesus Do?" Charles Shelton's 1898 book, *In His Steps*, introduced the Social Gospel teaching to a wide audience, selling more than 15 million copies. The Social Gospel Movement also spilled over into economics, with the prominent economist Richard Ely characterizing economics as a branch of Christian ethics. His book, *Social Aspects of Christianity* (1889), saw Christianity as "primarily concerned with this world," and argued in favor of labor unions, progressive taxation, and "socialization" of monopolies. Perhaps the most significant minister involved in the Social Gospel Movement was Walter Rauschenbusch, who published several major books on the Social Gospel between 1907 and 1917, the most famous of which was *Christianity and the Social Crisis* (1907). Rauschenbusch advocated a communitarian vision of society rejecting individualism in favor of "the next great principle" of "association."

The fifth and final element in the Progressive coalition was comprised of politicians. United by a belief in an activist government, these politicians were otherwise quite diverse, and often disagreed on specifics, particularly in the areas of economics and business, as we will review in detail below. Progressive politicians could be found on the local, state and national levels. Local Progressive politicians often directed their efforts towards specific issues which arose in their local areas, such as the Galveston and Dayton floods. Nationally, Progressive Parties emerged as third-party presidential contenders in both 1912 and 1924.

In addition to the legislation detailed in this chapter, the Progressive Movement was successful in its efforts to secure the passage and ratification of the Sixteenth through Nineteenth Amendments from 1913 to 1920. These provided, respectively, for imposition of an income tax, direct popular election of United States Senators, Prohibition, and Women's Suffrage. On the state level, Progressives were instrumental in securing passage of legislation providing for vehicles through which "the people" could secure reform, including the initiative, referendum, and recall of public officers.

Progressive Social Programs

While this work focuses on the growth and regulation of business enterprises, the Progressive approach to business regulation can best be understood in the context of its overall approach, including the social programs most Progressives supported. Here, again, the unifying vision was one of imposing structure and order on a diverse and changing society. "Good," as the Progressives saw it, was to be legislated, and structure and order imposed from above. Five examples will illustrate the Progressive approach to social issues.

Eugenics. Most Progressive politicians and Protestant clergy from the Social Gospel Movement were strong proponents of eugenics. Derived from the Greek word for "well-born," eugenics aimed at "purifying" the white race specifically, and society generally, by forced sterilization of "defectives" such as the blind and the deaf, as well as of the "homeless, tramps, and paupers." Thirty states passed forced sterilization laws, and some 20,000 people were sterilized under these laws. Most of the sterilizations occurred in California and Virginia, and Virginia's law was upheld as constitutional by the Supreme Court of the United States in *Buck v. Bell* (1927). Justice Oliver Wendell Holmes' opinion for all but one dissenting member of the Supreme Court opined that "It is better for all the world, if instead of waiting to execute degenerate offspring for crime, or to let them starve for their imbecility, society can prevent those who are manifestly unfit from continuing their kind....Three generations of imbeciles are enough." Holmes wrote to a British friend that this decision made him feel that "I was getting near the first principle of real reform."

Segregation. While the progeny of the targets of eugenics could be eliminated through forced sterilization, the existing African-American population could not. But in the minds of their leaders, Progressives believed that racial fears demanded a Progressive solution to maintain order between white and black, and to protect the weaker blacks from white rage. Segregation provided the necessary structure to assure the maintenance of order. As they were shielded behind racial walls, blacks could also be more easily controlled. As Michael McGerr has observed, "Most of the Progressives told themselves that separation allowed reform to continue. Protected by the shield of segregation, the fundamental prospect of transforming people could go on in safety."

Immigration. While the Progressive vision sought the complete elimination of "defectives" and the segregation of blacks from white society, this "purification" needed to be complemented by the exclusion of many would-be immigrants from Europe who sought refuge in the United States. In Progressive thinking, immigrants from Asia, as well as those from southern and eastern Europe, were inferior. Theodore Roosevelt certainly thought so. He saw Italians as the "most fecund and least desirable population of Europe," and considered the 1891 lynching of eleven Italian-Americans in New Orleans to be "a rather good thing." Woodrow Wilson shared these views. In his *History of the American People*, Wilson wrote about "the coarse crew that came crowding in every year at the eastern ports." Similarly, E.A. Ross, a prominent sociologist of the times, saw southern and eastern Europeans as "beaten members of beaten breeds." Given these views, it is not surprising that Progressives supported harsh restrictions on immigration. For example, the National Origins Act of 1924 limited admission to the United States based on the numbers of individuals of particular nationalities residing in the United States in 1890. 1890 was selected because it predated the mass immigration of peoples from southern and eastern Europe.

Prohibition. The winnowing fans of eugenics, segregation, and restrictions on immigration still left the Progressives with the problem they perceived of dealing with those lower classes who remained in the country. Prohibition, enforced throughout the country under the authority of the Eighteenth Amendment, was one answer. A motivating factor in Progressive support for Prohibition was social control. Progressives saw African-Americans, as well as Irish and German immigrants, as threats to social order. Cutting off their alcohol would, in the Progressives' view, help to control them. This fear was also a motivating factor for imposing Sunday "Blue Laws" which closed taverns and other public places on Sundays, segregating feared groups from society on their day of rest. Looking at the Progressives' record in this area, James Morone observed that "Going dry was the city on the hill at its most ambitious. But dry dreams kept getting tangled up in racial fears."

Public Education. Controlling the immigrant Catholic and Jewish population was an additional aim of Progressive legislation regulating the schooling of children. In order to "Americanize" foreign immigrant children of non-Protestant faiths, Progressives supported compulsory public education, and special juvenile courts to deal with the unruly. Not satisfied with these measures, Oregon Progressives (with the support of the Ku Klux Klan) secured the enactment of a law, which was ratified in a statewide referendum, requiring that all normal children between the ages of eight and 16 be educated exclusively in the public schools of that state, thus eliminating education offered by religious and private schools. This alliance of the Klan with these Progressives has been aptly characterized as "hooded Progressivism." Their efforts failed, however, when the

Supreme Court declared the Oregon law unconstitutional in *Pierce v. The Society of Sisters* (1925).

Progressive Views on Business Regulation.

While Progressives generally supported the social programs discussed above, there was less agreement, and substantial variation, in their approaches to regulation of business enterprises. Once again, however, there was a shared recognition that structure and order needed to be imposed upon business enterprises by government intervention through regulation. Thus, the common theme among Progressive politicians was to "give the government more power in business affairs," as Ray Stannard Baker had put it, or to "civilize industry," in the words of Henry Demarest Lloyd, an urban Populist. But there were significant differences as to the proper approach to business regulation. These differences are readily apparent in the policies pursued by the three men who served as president in the first 20 years of the twentieth century. As outlined below, the two Republican presidents, Theodore Roosevelt and William Howard Taft, differed not only from Woodrow Wilson, the Democrat, but also between themselves, on how best to regulate business.

Theodore Roosevelt: Controlling the "Malefactors of Great Wealth"

Theodore Roosevelt was an accidental president. Serving as vice president, he assumed the office of president only as a result of the assassination of President McKinley in September of 1901, six months into McKinley's second term. Mark Hanna, a business-friendly senator who had managed McKinley's campaigns, made the famous remark that that "damned cowboy" had become president.

Roosevelt has been variously praised or vilified by historians and commentators for inaugurating a more activist federal government. It is certainly true that his philosophy of government was consistent with this goal. In his autobiography, Roosevelt wrote that he "was bent upon making the Government the most efficient possible instrument in helping the people of the United States to better themselves in every way, politically, socially, and industrially." In reality, however, Charles Beard correctly noted that his legislative accomplishments were modest. As Beard put it, "the social legislation passed during Mister Roosevelt's administrations is not very extensive, although it was accompanied by much discussion at the time." Part of the explanation for this stems from the fact that President Roosevelt was engaged in a wide variety of national and international issues which consumed much of his time. These issues included resolving the war between Russia and Japan, which led to his being awarded the Nobel Peace Prize in 1906; settling the Anthracite Strike of 1902; negotiating with Colombia and Panama to build the Panama Canal; and dealing with threats to peace in Venezuela and Cuba.

Roosevelt did achieve some substantial legislative accomplishments in the area of business regulation. To address the predatory power of railroads, he secured the enactment of two major pieces of legislation. The Elkins

Act of 1903 prohibited railroads from granting rebates to large volume shippers, an issue which had been highlighted by the Populists, while the Hepburn Act of 1906 authorized the Interstate Commerce Commission to set maximum freight and passenger rates and extended the ICC's authority to oil pipelines, express companies, and dockyards. The latter legislation also permitted federal authorities to inspect railroad records and prescribed uniform bookkeeping rules.

In his second term, Roosevelt capitalized on the publicity generated by Upton Sinclair's muckraking novel, *The Jungle*, to secure the passage of the Meat Inspection Law, which authorized federal inspectors to enforce sanitary regulations in meat packing operations. On the same day in 1906, Congress also passed the Pure Food and Drug Act, which prohibited the shipment in interstate commerce of adulterated or mislabeled foods, drugs, and alcoholic drinks. Enactment of these two federal laws greatly expanded the reach of the federal government in areas which previously had been regulated by the states.

While the railroad, meat packing, and food and drug laws were limited to specific industries, Roosevelt had a broader vision regarding the appropriate way to control business excesses. In 1903, he was able to establish a Department of Commerce and Labor with a Bureau of Corporations which was designed to investigate corporate wrongdoing. In his autobiography, Roosevelt stated that "I have always believed that it would also be necessary to give the National Government *complete power* over the organization and capitalization of all business

concerns engaged in interstate commerce." He therefore contended, repeatedly but unsuccessfully, for the
establishment of a commission "covering the whole
field of interstate business, exclusive of transportation
…" Concluding that the antitrust laws were ineffective
to restrain corporate abuses, he argued for "thoroughgo-
ing administrative control by the Government," which
would exercise "a steady expert control" because large
corporations required "close and jealous supervision."
In his view, "The power of the mighty industrial over-
lords of the country had increased with great strides,
while the methods of controlling them, or checking
abuses by them, on the part of the people, through the
Government, remained archaic and therefore practically
impotent."

Despite these views, Roosevelt did not believe that
all large corporations should be broken up; in his 1904
Message to Congress, he expressed the view that "combination and concentration should be, not prohibited,
but supervised and within reasonable limits controlled."
This fit well with Roosevelt's Manichaean view of the
corporate world. While denigrating the effectiveness of
the antitrust laws because they required long, drawn-
out, and expensive litigation, he nevertheless utilized
the Sherman Act to break up what he considered to be
"bad" trusts run by "predatory wealth." He reasoned
that in the world of trusts there was a "wide difference in
the moral obliquity indicated by the wrongdoer." In his
autobiography, he stated that "The effort to prohibit all
combinations, good or bad, is bound to fail, and ought to
fail; when made, it merely means that some of the worst

combinations are not checked and that honest business is checked." He sought to explain his antitrust policy by contending that "the corporations against we proceeded had *sinned*, not merely by being big (which we did not regard as in itself a sin), but by being guilty of unfair practices toward their competitors, and by procuring [unfair] advantages from the railways."

Roosevelt's antitrust suits were based upon moral judgments directed against those he considered to be "malefactors of great wealth." His biographer Louis Auchincloss concluded that Roosevelt "wanted not so much to raise the poor as to lower the proud." Several remarks in Roosevelt's autobiography reflect this approach. For example, Roosevelt claimed that "When I took the presidency, it was a common and bitter saying that a big man, a rich man, could not be put in jail. We put many big and rich men in jail."

Roosevelt's most significant antitrust prosecution was directed against the formation of the Northern Securities Company, which would have been the second largest corporation in the world. Northern Securities was a holding company which combined the Great Northern, the Northern Pacific, and the Chicago, Burlington & Quincy railroads into one integrated operation in seventeen separate states. The principal actors in the formation of the holding company were J.P. Morgan, James J. Hill, and E.H. Harriman, all of whom were exceedingly wealthy corporate leaders of the time. In its five to four decision in *Northern Securities Co. v. United States* (1904), the Supreme Court of United States held that the combination was illegal. In his plurality opinion for four members of the court, Justice John Marshall Harlan concluded that the stock acquired by the holding company "was acquired and held to be used in suppressing competition between those companies. It came into existence only for that purpose."

Roosevelt had two reactions to his narrow victory in the Supreme Court. He first noted that "the most powerful men in the country were held to accountability before the law." But he also recorded his disappointment in the dissenting opinion filed by his appointee to the court, Justice Oliver Wendell Holmes, about whom he was quite dismissive. As Roosevelt put it, "I could carve out of a banana a judge with more backbone than that."

The *Northern Securities* case presented a confrontation between business and government, and J. P. Morgan was gravely disappointed that Roosevelt had chosen to litigate the matter rather than to negotiate an amicable resolution. Three years later, however, Morgan would cooperate with the Roosevelt Administration to end the Panic of 1907. That Panic had its roots in excess speculation in stocks by trust companies, which lent vast sums collateralized by stocks in heavily margined accounts. The trust companies lacked financial discipline and failed to follow the sound banking practices implemented by commercial banks.

The immediate cause of the 1907 Panic was the total collapse in October of the stock price of United Copper, a large corporation which had been the target of an attempt to corner its stock by the company's founder and other speculators financed by the Knickerbocker Trust Company. When the stock price collapsed, so did

Knickerbocker when its depositors began a run on the trust company which ended in its demise when its funds were totally depleted. The collapse of Knickerbocker catalyzed runs on other financial institutions, whose depositors ran to reclaim their funds. This led to those institutions calling other margined loans, further depressing the price of the stocks which were pledged as collateral. To stem the tide, J.P. Morgan worked with the Roosevelt Administration to raise $40 million to place on deposit in the affected banks. Roosevelt's Treasury Secretary, George Cortelyou, assisted in this effort by providing $25 million of government funds to be used at Morgan's discretion to assist the affected financial institutions. This combined private and public funding ended the immediate crisis.

In a second phase of the Panic of 1907, brokers on the New York Stock Exchange ran out of money to continue trading. Morgan again stemmed the tide by raising $25 million to enable trading to continue, thus restoring confidence in the exchange.

The third and final episode in the 1907 Panic came in November, when the brokerage house of Moore & Schley was about to fail, staggering under a debt load of some $25 million. Moore & Schley then had a large interest in the stock of Tennessee Coal and Iron Company, which was a competitor of U.S. Steel. In order to save Moore & Schley from bankruptcy, Morgan arranged for U.S. Steel to purchase Tennessee Coal and Iron. To implement this U.S. Steel purchase of its competitor, Morgan needed to obtain an antitrust waiver from the Roosevelt Administration. Morgan's representatives therefore met with President Roosevelt personally, and obtained assurances from him that his Administration would not challenge the U.S. Steel purchase in court.

In exchange for his assistance to Moore & Schley, and in a further effort to stabilize the economy, Morgan also insisted upon a *quid pro quo* from executives of several trust companies. He successfully importuned them to establish a pool of $25 million to assist troubled trust companies.

The cooperative efforts of business and government in resolving the Panic of 1907 illustrate just how valuable that cooperation can be. The role played by Morgan, however, placed a bright light on the need for what became the Federal Reserve System, a topic discussed later in this chapter. After 1913, no longer would a private businessman or woman play the role the 70 year old, semi-retired, J. P. Morgan did in 1907.

William Howard Taft: The Rule of Law

The presidency of William Howard Taft, a one-term president who served between 1909 and 1913, is often viewed by historians as a quiet interlude and mere footnote between the presidencies of Theodore Roosevelt and Woodrow Wilson. Like Herbert Hoover after him, Taft was highly qualified to be president based on an extensive prior history of public service. But, again like Hoover, Taft lacked the common touch manifested by most successful politicians, and thereby failed in his presidential reelection effort in 1912. He finished third in that election, carrying only two states.

Taft was Theodore Roosevelt's chosen successor.

Prior to the presidency, he had performed with distinction in a number of posts, including federal appeals judge, United States Solicitor General, Governor General of the Philippines, and Roosevelt's Secretary of War. Eventually, he would serve as Chief Justice of the United States -- the only person ever to serve in the highest position in both the executive and judicial branches.

In his 1909 Inaugural Address, Taft pledged to maintain and enforce Roosevelt's reforms, and to further expand them through amendments to the federal antitrust laws and to the laws governing interstate commerce. Taft recognized in his address that "The scope of a modern government in what it can and ought to accomplish for its people" had "widened far beyond the principles laid down by the old 'laissez-faire' school of political writers." But Taft also emphasized the importance of an even-handed application of the laws through the courts. He further recognized the need to assure "American business...of that measure of stability and certainty in respect to those things that may be done and those that are prohibited which is essential to the life and growth of all business." With respect to the trust problem, Taft somewhat echoed Roosevelt, reminding his listeners of the need for "differentiating between combinations based upon legitimate economic reasons and those formed with the intent of creating monopolies and artificially controlling prices."

Taft's Administration had three major initiatives in the area of business regulation. First, he saw the antitrust laws as a valuable tool to combat the predatory practices of large corporations, and, unlike Theodore

Roosevelt, trusted the courts to enforce those laws. In his autobiography, Roosevelt characterized the courts as having been "for a quarter of a century...on the whole the agents of reaction." Taft, by contrast, saw his fellow judges as "high priests in the temple of justice," and considered attacks on the Supreme Court by Roosevelt and other Progressives as seeking to "lay the axe at the root tree of our civilization."

Taft implemented his views by filing many more antitrust suits in his four years in office than Roosevelt had done in his seven years. While commentators differ on just how many suits each president filed to enforce the antitrust laws, it is generally agreed that Taft filed between two and three times more suits than Roosevelt had done. Taft even sued United States Steel, which Roosevelt had seen as a "good" trust.

A second subject to which Taft devoted a great deal of attention was the protective tariff, which had long been a staple of Republican Platforms. Taft had the platform changed to call for a revision of the tariff system. His view was that tariffs should be limited to an amount representing the differential between "the cost of production abroad and at home." Such a limitation would protect consumers from being overcharged and make it more difficult for a domestic producer to obtain or maintain a monopoly. Taft's efforts to reform the tariff system were supported by articles written by Ida Tarbell, who documented how the tariff system then in place had generated excessive profits for monopolists and higher prices for consumers.

Despite Taft's tariff reform initiatives and Tarbell's

articles, tariff revision faced strong opposition in the United States Senate, led by Senator Nelson Aldrich of Rhode Island. While the House of Representatives passed a bill which reduced many tariff duties, Aldrich undid most of the important reforms in his Senate proposal. After much back and forth, the ultimate Payne-Aldrich Tariff legislation restored many of the cuts demanded by Taft and he signed the bill although he conceded that it was not a "perfect" resolution of the tariff issue, recognizing that duties on important consumer products such as cotton and wool were not reduced, and in some cases were actually increased. In the face of strong Progressive opposition to the ultimate Payne-Aldrich Tariff, and in an attempt to advance party unity, Taft made the mistake of calling the Payne-Aldrich legislation "the best bill that the Republican party ever passed." Instead of uniting the party, this drove a reform-minded Progressive Republican faction further away from Taft, and paved the way for Theodore Roosevelt to run against Taft in the election of 1912.

Taft's third major effort was in the area of railroad regulation. He successfully obtained passage of the Mann-Elkins Act in 1910. That legislation conferred power on the Interstate Commerce Commission to delay railroad rate changes, and to regulate telegraph, telephone and wireless companies. The legislation also established a special Commerce Court to facilitate speedier rulings; that court, however, was abolished by Congress in 1913.

In the final analysis, Taft proved himself to be an exponent of limited and incremental law-based reform.

"Good," in his opinion, could not simply be legislated. Instead, his view was that "The lesson must be learned that there is only a limited zone within which legislation and governments can accomplish good." This traditional, conservative view was inconsistent with the Progressive vision of reconstructing society and led to Taft's defeat in the immensely significant election of 1912, where four competing views of business regulation were publicly debated at great length and with intense vigor.

The Election of 1912

Four major candidates competed for the presidency in 1912. These included the incumbent Republican, President Taft; former president Theodore Roosevelt, who campaigned as the candidate of the new Progressive Party; Woodrow Wilson, previously the governor of New Jersey and the president of Princeton University, who ran as the Democratic candidate; and Eugene Debs, the former labor leader, who ran as a Socialist.

The election soon became a two-way contest between Roosevelt and Wilson. The ex-president regretted his previous decision not to seek a third term in 1908, and felt that Taft had abandoned the Progressive cause by surrendering to "the great privileged interests." Roosevelt was also angered when Taft filed an antitrust suit against U.S. Steel, suggesting that Roosevelt had been deceived when he indicated he would not prosecute that corporation for its acquisition of Tennessee Coal & Iron.

Roosevelt campaigned on a platform of the "New

Nationalism," calling for a strong federal government to protect society. In an early 1910 speech at Osawatomie, Kansas, he declared that "every man holds his property subject to the general right of the community to regulate its use to whatever degree the public welfare may require it." While such a view had been articulated years before by Chief Justice Waite in the famous Granger case of *Munn v. Illinois* (1877), it was seen as radical by mainline Republicans and business interests. Roosevelt was viewed even more harshly by his party for his repeated attacks on the judiciary, calling for the recall of unpopular decisions rendered by state court judges.

Despite his victory in many of the Republican primaries, Roosevelt was denied the Republican nomination in 1912 in a stacked convention which renominated Taft. Within days Roosevelt received the nomination of the Progressive Party, whose delegates were mainly well-educated, middle-class business and medical professionals and educators, both male and female. One of his staunchest supporters, who seconded his nomination, was Jane Addams, one of the earliest Progressives. The Progressive convention was conducted with high energy in a heavily moral and religious atmosphere. Roosevelt's acceptance speech closed with the rallying cry that "We stand at Armageddon, and we battle for the Lord." The convention itself ended with the delegates singing "Praise God from whom all blessings flow."

In the 1912 campaign, Roosevelt promised to "use the whole power of government to protect those who… are trodden down in the ferocious scrambling rush of an unregulated and purely individualistic industrialism."

In his view, "only by the power of government can we curb the greed that sits in high places." Roosevelt called yet again for the establishment of a "national industrial commission" which would regulate all corporations involved in interstate commerce, other than transportation companies. He also continued to distinguish between "good" and "bad" trusts, contrasting natural growth with growth attained through unethical practices. His commission would set maximum prices and even review the wages and hours of labor. In sum, his approach called for less prosecution of large corporations in favor of more intense regulation.

Wilson also campaigned against the trusts, calling for a "New Freedom." Reflecting the influence of Louis Brandeis, the "People's Lawyer" whom Wilson would later nominate for the Supreme Court, Wilson called for the destruction of the trusts, both "good" and "bad," in order to restore true competition. In Wilson's view, the war against the trusts represented "a second struggle for emancipation."

Wilson rejected the Progressive approach, which he characterized as favoring "government by experts." He also called for a smaller federal government than that favored by Roosevelt, contending that issues such as those relating to wages and hours and the conditions of labor should be left to the states. Moreover, in place of the specific and intensive regulation of large corporations favored by Roosevelt, Wilson called instead for the enactment of general "remedial legislation" which would set the bounds of competition for all corporations. In his view, "We are not fighting the trusts, we are trying to put them upon an equality with everybody else."

While Roosevelt and Wilson both campaigned vigorously, Taft was lethargic and depressed, feeling certain that he would be defeated by his former good friend Roosevelt. From time to time, however, Taft attacked Roosevelt's "New Nationalism" and compared the Progressives to the extremists of the French Revolution. Indeed, he called Roosevelt a "demagogue" and a "dangerous egoist" driven by "personal ambition." In addition, Taft continued to believe that antitrust prosecutions before experienced judges were preferable to Roosevelt's industrial commission.

The Socialist candidate, Eugene Debs, attacked the trusts and all industrial corporations with more vigor than Wilson or even Roosevelt. Debs sought "mastery and control of industry," and, reflecting the Populist Platform of the 1890s, favored nationalization of key industries, including transportation, communications, and banking.

Each of the four candidates drew substantial popular support, but when Taft and Roosevelt split the old Republican vote, Wilson emerged triumphant with almost 6.3 million votes, representing nearly 42 percent of the total popular vote and 435 electoral votes. Roosevelt finished second, a remarkable showing for a third party candidate. He obtained 4.1 million votes, over 27 percent of the total popular vote, with 88 electoral votes. Taft finished third, winning nearly 3.5 million votes, representing over 23 percent of the total; he won only two states with eight electoral votes. Debs won 900,000 votes, six percent of the total popular vote, the largest vote ever for this perennial socialist candidate. Indeed, in the states of Texas, Oklahoma, and Nevada, he took sixteen percent of the popular vote.

Roosevelt and Taft received a combined vote total of more than 50 percent, enough to have defeated Wilson if one candidate could have held that total vote. Nevertheless, it is notable that a large majority of the electorate favored some sort of progressive reform, since Wilson and Roosevelt took some 70 percent of the popular vote. Thus, while it is possible that Roosevelt could have been elected president if he had obtained the Republican nomination, Taft probably could not have done so.

Woodrow Wilson and the Rise of Federal Power

Woodrow Wilson's presidency marked the high point of the Progressive Movement before the New Deal. To begin with, although the legislative work for the first two was begun under the Republicans who preceded Wilson, four constitutional amendments were ratified by the states between Wilson's 1913 election and the end of his second term in 1920. These amendments were the first to be ratified since the aftermath of the Civil War, and implemented core parts of the Progressive platform -- an income tax, direct election of senators, prohibition, and women's suffrage.

Wilson also secured the passage of several key pieces of legislation, most of which were enacted in the first 18 months of his first term. These fall into four areas: tariff reform; banking regulation; antitrust legislation;

and farm relief. Each piece of legislation, as well as the four constitutional amendments, sought to implement the Progressive goal of imposing a proper structure and order on society.

Tariff reform had long been a key plank in Democratic platforms following the Civil War, and represented the key difference between Republicans and Democrats in the last third of the nineteenth century. The 1913 Underwood-Simmons Tariff gave the Democrats their long-sought victory, reducing the tariff from an average of 37 percent on imported goods to approximately 27 percent. Tariffs on nearly 1000 articles, including important consumer goods such as wool and even farming equipment, were either reduced or completely eliminated. Significantly, although tariff reduction was presented as a trust-busting measure to protect the consumer from monopoly pricing, the larger businesses which by that time were established in their market positions were less concerned with these tariff reductions than were smaller businesses, which felt that the tariff protected them and that tariff reduction or elimination might lead to their demise from foreign competition.

In order to make up the lost revenues from widespread tariff reductions, the Wilson Administration enacted the first federal income tax. This imposed a tax rate of 1 percent on all incomes above $4000, an income level which only two percent of workers attained at the time. The rates rose to a maximum of seven percent on incomes exceeding $1 million, implementing the Progressive view that any income tax should be leveled on a progressive basis, taxing higher earners at a higher rate.

With respect to banking, Wilson's most important legislative achievement was enactment of the Federal Reserve Act in 1913. In 1911, Wilson had expressed the view that "The great monopoly in this country is the money monopoly," with the large New York banks epitomized by J.P. Morgan controlling the money supply. The Panic of 1907 gave credence in Progressive eyes to this view. The Federal Reserve Act was a compromise measure which sought to limit the power of the New York banking establishment, and to balance overall control of the money supply by the federal government with regional implementation of policy. To that end, the Federal Reserve was empowered to set interest rates to control the money supply through a structure which included twelve regional banks. Federal Reserve notes became a new medium of currency backed by a 40 percent gold reserve and short-term commercial paper. Previously, the money supply had been tied to gold or United States bonds, which restricted the supply of money. By providing the structure for increasing the money supply, Wilson addressed a key concern of the old Populist Movement.

In addition to achieving tariff and tax reform and establishing a new system of banking regulation, Wilson also secured passage of two new antitrust laws to strengthen government power to stop monopolistic and other predatory practices. Wilson took a belt and suspenders approach with separate legislation first addressing specific anti-competitive practices, and next empowering government to identify and enjoin other unfair devices and schemes.

The first law, the Clayton Act of 1914, reflected Wilson's view that anticompetitive practices "can be explicitly and item by item forbidden by statute in such terms as will practically eliminate uncertainty." The practices banned by the Clayton Act included (1) interlocking directorships, which had been employed to confer power on a small group of individuals, including J. P. Morgan, to control large portions of American industry, including actual and potential competitors, by placing their designees on multiple corporate boards; (2) price discrimination, which favored and further concentrated power in large industries benefited by the lower prices extracted by them to the detriment of their smaller competitors; (3) the tying of different products together for sale, a practice which required the customer to buy both products in order to obtain the desired commodity and thus limited consumer choice and permitted companies with a desirable product to force customers to buy a less desirable product against their will; and (4) mergers and stock acquisitions which substantially lessened competition or tended to create a monopoly, another legislative response to the continuing concentration taking place in American industry at the time.

Once again, demonstrating that business was (and is) not a monolith politically, many businesses welcomed such legislation since it established one set of rules for all competitors, curbed the power of market leaders, and led to predictability and stability in business operations.

While the Clayton Act *banned* specific practices deemed to be anticompetitive, the Federal Trade Commission Act of 1914 sought to *regulate* the practices of all businesses affecting interstate commerce in order to end other anticompetitive practices which might be devised by corporations to unfairly attain or enhance market power. To this end, a new commission similar to that long favored by Theodore Roosevelt was established with the commissioners authorized to define and attack any practices which they, as purported experts, deemed to constitute "unfair methods of competition." Once this Federal Trade Commission had identified that a particular corporation had engaged in methods of competition which were deemed to be unfair, the commission was empowered to issue cease-and-desist orders. The FTC used this discretionary power often in its early days, issuing some 379 orders during Wilson's presidency. This unbridled and unpredictable power fostered uncertainty and, unlike the Clayton Act, made doing business more difficult, hanging a damoclean sword over all businesses.

In 1916, the Wilson Administration turned its focus to the farming community, with two pieces of reform legislation directed at the old Populist heartland. The Federal Farm Loan Act of that year established a system for agricultural lending which paralleled that set up by the Federal Reserve Act. Once again a centralized Federal Farm Loan Bank was complemented by twelve regional banks. Loans were authorized to be made to farmers in amounts up to 70 percent of the value of their land, buildings, and improvements, and for terms ranging between five and 40 years. Interest rates were capped at six percent. The second law addressing the agricultural community was the Warehouse Act of 1916. This permitted the federal agency to issue receipts, which were negotiable instruments, to farmers for their crops, enabling them to cash in before those crops were actually sold. The legislation enacted a variation of the old Populist scheme popularized by Charles Macune for a "subtreasury" which would assist farmers.

These accomplishments by Wilson in his first term justified his 1916 pronouncement that "We have in four years come very close to carrying out the platform of the Progressive party as well as our own; for we also are progressives." But the advent of World War I would soon turn the country's attention to the involvement of the United States in that conflict. Preparing for war resulted in a resurgence of big business, with a concomitant movement toward greater concentration in key industries.

CHAPTER FIVE
FROM CONFRONTATION TO COOPERATION: WORLD WAR I, BUSINESS, AND THE RETURN OF REPUBLICAN RULE

World War I and the Business-Government Partnership

World War I generated a fundamental change in the approach of the Wilson Administration to the regulation of business. Confrontation was replaced by cooperation. While Wilson as a candidate and in the first few years of his presidency had sought to break up big businesses, Wilson the commander-in-chief needed the assistance of business to support the war effort in World War I. While the war years saw an expansion of federal power, that expansion was undertaken in a cooperative effort with business. As David Kennedy has properly observed, during this period and into the 1920s, there was "a marked shift toward corporatism in the nation's business affairs."

The demands of war created new markets and

increased profits for American business and further catalyzed its growth. The costs of the war effort were enormous, reaching some $33 billion. The United States Armed Forces grew from 100,000 to 5,000,000 in one year, and those soldiers had to be fed, clothed, housed, supported, and armed. Women were employed in large numbers to support the war effort, with one million hired to replace men who were serving in the military. Farmers also profited. The Allied demand for food to replace that which had been grown on European farms now ravaged by war led the United States government to guarantee high prices for agricultural products, which in turn prompted farmers to expand their output. Price McKinney, a steel executive, gave business' view of the war when he observed that "We are all making more money out of this war than the average human being ought to."

On the government side, World War I saw the creation of multiple new federal agencies designed to assist the war effort. One such agency, begun in 1917, was the War Industries Board which sought to allocate scarce resources, maximize production, and standardize American products. The Board reflected the Progressive view of imposing structure and order by seeking to achieve rationality through combination. Its head, Wall Street financier Bernard Baruch, saw the Board as pointing to "the desirability of investing some Government agency…with… powers… to encourage, under strict Government supervision, such cooperation and coordination in industry as should tend to increase production, eliminate waste, conserve natural resources, improve the quality of products, promote efficiency in operation, and thus reduce costs to the ultimate consumer."

Given such a view, it is not surprising that the antitrust laws championed by President Wilson were rarely enforced since they were viewed as an obstacle to structuring business to assist in the war effort. Attorney General Thomas Gregory later admitted that "We let the cases go to sleep until the war was over." Indeed, expenditures on antitrust enforcement declined by a factor of nearly three and one-half times, decreasing from $270,000 in 1914 to $81,000 in 1919. Cooperation was the new template, and the Chamber of Commerce aptly observed that "war is the stern teacher that is driving home the lesson of cooperative effort."

That cooperative effort affected all aspects of business. The War Industries Board set prices for industrial production, and businesses were told exactly what to produce. By the establishment of high prices and the awarding of contracts on a cost-plus basis, the Board's approach benefited large, low-cost businesses and facilitated mergers and other combinations which Wilson the candidate had vigorously opposed. The Board also standardized some 30,000 industrial and consumer products. To take just a few examples, auto tire sizes were reduced from 287 to nine; typewriter ribbon colors were reduced from 150 to five; and the types of pocket knives were reduced from 6000 to 144. Uniform standards were also imposed for items such as baby carriages, and the use of tin in toy carts was prohibited, in order to save some 75,000 tons of tin for use in the war effort. The nation's railroads, shipbuilders, and communications were also coordinated through a government takeover. Under a Railroad Administration led by William Gibbs McAdoo, Wilson's Secretary of the Treasury and son-in-law, competing railroad operations were coordinated into a single national system to impose structure and order. Railroad terminals were combined; uniform standards were imposed for railroad equipment; and low traffic lines were eliminated. Railroad owners were well-compensated in this co-operative effort with railroad rates fixed at a high level, and the railroads guaranteed a favorable return on their investment.

A Fuel Administration was also established to regulate such items as the production and consumption of coal. "Fuelless Mondays" and daylight savings time were begun to save fuel for the military effort. To secure the cooperation of labor and to avoid strikes which would damage the war effort, a National War Labor Board pressured companies through a pro-labor dispute resolution mechanism to pay minimum wages and to follow an eight-hour day. The Board demonstrated the seriousness of its efforts by taking over the weapons manufacturer Smith & Wesson when it rejected one of the Board's rulings.

The Food Administration, led by future president Herbert Hoover, was another significant new federal agency. It encouraged fasting from meat, wheat and other staples on specific week days. Hoover's approach was cooperative and voluntary. He stated that he sought to "mobilize the spirit of self-denial and self-sacrifice" to conserve food for the Allied forces. As such, the Food Administration did not impose rationing or other compulsory mechanisms. Once again, this agency fostered a cooperative effort between government and business by setting, for example, high prices through local Farm Bureaus to assure that farmers would produce sufficient food for the Allied forces in Europe, and by agreeing to buy all unsold farm production. While the Administration also regulated profits, it did so only after consultation with the Farm Bureaus.

To finance the extensive and expensive war effort, the Wilson Administration raised the rates on the federal income tax. In the 1916 Revenue Act, taxes were doubled on the top 13 percent; they were further increased in 1917 and 1918 by which time the top rate reached 77 percent. Inheritance taxes were also imposed as an additional source of financing. By war's end, 75 percent of government funding came from taxes; before World War I, 75 percent had come from tariffs, the rates on which Wilson had reduced in his first term.

World War I provided a preview of a large federal government regulating major aspects of American life. The approach taken in these early efforts, by contrast to some of those implemented later, incorporated a cooperative effort between government and business. With the end of World War I, and the return of Republican rule in the 1920s, this relationship between business and government remained a close and cooperative one.

The Republican 1920s: Continued Business-Government Cooperation

With the end of World War I, the Republican Party was restored to power in the election of 1920. Warren

Harding was elected president with an overwhelming 60 percent of the popular vote. He defeated the Democrat James Cox and his running mate Franklin Delano Roosevelt; the Democratic ticket received only 34 percent of the vote, with the Socialist candidate Eugene Debs picking up most of the remaining votes. Harding sought "not heroics but healing; not nostrums but normalcy," and promised to "free business from arbitrary and unnecessary control." In his inaugural address, Harding warned that "No alternate system will work a miracle. Any wild experiment will only add to the confusion." Instead, he sought to "speak for administrative efficiency, for lightened tax burdens, for adequate credit facilities, for sympathetic concern for all agricultural problems, for the omission of unnecessary interference of government with business, for an end to government's experiment in business, and for more efficient business in government administration."

After Harding died in office, his vice president, Calvin Coolidge, succeeded him. Coolidge thereafter won the presidency in his own right in the election of 1924, defeating both the Democratic candidate, John W. Davis, a Wall Street lawyer, and the Progressive Party candidate, Robert LaFollette, a United States senator from Wisconsin. Most voters repudiated the Progressive Party platform as the "wild experiment" Harding had spoken against. That platform called, among other things, for public ownership of water power; popular election of federal judges; congressional overruling of unpopular judicial opinions; abolition of the military draft; and a popular referendum on any declaration of war. While unsuccessful, the Progressive Party never-theless drew an impressive vote for a third party: one out of six voters chose LaFollette in 1924. The Democratic ticket headed by Davis received only 28.8 percent of the popular vote.

Republicans continued their electoral dominance in the election of 1928, when their candidate, Herbert Hoover, polled 58 percent of the vote against the Democratic candidate Alfred Smith, who took only 41 percent of the vote, losing many votes because of his Catholic religion.

The economy was in bad shape when Harding assumed the presidency in 1921, much of which was attributable to the disappearance of the booming, but evanescent, war economy. In 1920, the economy had shrunk some 20 percent, and unemployment stood at 10 percent. With their return to power, Republicans in the 1920s set about undoing many of Wilson's initiatives, and returned to many facets of their pro-business nineteenth century platform, largely abandoning the Progressive impulses of Roosevelt and Taft, with the notable exception of the wing of the party led by the aforementioned Senator Robert LaFollette. The main branch of the Republican Party, however, restored a tariff system protective of American business; implemented tax cuts; lessened government spending; and introduced programs which encouraged the growth of a powerful industrial economy led by large corporations.

Wilson's tariff reductions were partially reversed in the Fordney-McCumber Tariff of 1922, and more conclusively in the infamous Hawley-Smoot Tariff of 1930, which established the highest tariffs yet, and restored protections against foreign competition to American businesses. Next, taxes were reduced under President Calvin Coolidge through policies instituted by Secretary of the Treasury Andrew Mellon. Mellon, formerly a Pittsburgh banker and still one of the richest men in the country in the 1920s, was the longest-serving Treasury Secretary in history, serving in that position under all three Republican presidents elected in that decade. He believed in "scientific taxation," calculating that lowering tax rates would actually increase tax revenues. Mellon's plan to reduce tax rates met vigorous opposition from Progressives and others, and he achieved only partial successes in the early tax-reform legislation of the 1920s. Mellon nevertheless persevered, and he was finally victorious in achieving many of his tax-cutting goals in the Revenue Act of 1926. Significantly, even while reducing taxes, Mellon was also able to reduce the national debt from its all-time high of $24 billion at the end of World War I to $19.6 million in 1926, and then to $16 million in 1930.

To assist business more directly, President Coolidge called for "reducing" government agencies which regulated "business activities," and he therefore cut their budgets. In addition, Republican Administrations in the 1920s continued to permit, and even to promote, business mergers and other combinations. From 1919 to 1929, 10,000 companies either disappeared or were swallowed up in some 1268 combinations, an average of approximately 1000 firms lost each year. The resulting concentration of corporate power was manifested by the fact that in 1933, 594 corporations owned 53 percent of all domestic assets, leaving the other 387,974 corporations with the remaining 47 percent. By the 1930s, J.P. Morgan's interests alone controlled some $74 billion in assets through interlocking directorates and other corporate arrangements, which was possible only because banks had been exempted from the Clayton Act prohibition on interlocking directorates. These Morgan interests represented approximately 25 percent of all corporate assets at that time.

Despite Harding's expressed concern for agriculture, that sector of the American economy suffered from changing economic conditions, including the end of inflated market prices caused by the shortages of World War I and the elimination of the European market for agricultural goods. By 1932, for example, cereal and cotton prices were only one third of what they had been in 1920.

The Supreme Court: Business' Safety Valve

As it had done in the last part of the nineteenth century, business resorted to the courts again to curb what it saw as overly intrusive regulation in the 1920s. Indeed, a combination of Republican Administration policies and Supreme Court decisions unfavorable to labor led to a decline in union membership. Union membership had increased under Wilson's war policies from approximately 3 million in 1917 to 5 million in 1920. By 1929, however, union membership had again decreased to less than 3 million.

The Supreme Court's approach to labor issues in the

Progressive Era had been somewhat contradictory. In the infamous case of *Lochner v. New York* (1905), the court struck down a New York law forbidding bakers to work more than 10 hours in any one day, or more than 60 hours in one week. A harshly divided court held this New York legislation unconstitutional because it interfered with "the general right to make a contract in relation to his business," a right which the majority found to be "part of the liberty of the individual protected by the 14th Amendment." *Lochner* was a serious defeat for unions which had supported the New York legislation in order to reduce competition from bakeries run by immigrants who worked longer hours and took business away from the larger corporate bakers which were unionized.

Lochner was at the time, and continues to be, harshly criticized, and the Supreme Court backtracked somewhat when it upheld two Oregon laws regulating maximum hours without repudiating *Lochner*. Thus, in *Muller v. Oregon* (1908), the court upheld a law limiting hours women could work in factories and similar establishments because of the importance of "healthy mothers" with "vigorous offspring." The court went further in *Bunting v. Oregon* (1917), by upholding a law prescribing a 10 hour day for mill, factory, and manufacturing workers, finding this legislation to be a reasonable health regulation.

After *Bunting*, the *Lochner* freedom of contract approach appeared to be on its last legs. The situation changed dramatically, however, when President Harding was able to nominate, and secure the confirmation of, four new justices, including former President

Taft as Chief Justice. This changed court revived the *Lochner* approach. Thus, in *Adkins v. Children's Hospital* (1923), a divided court struck down federal legislation establishing minimum wages for women and children working in the District of Columbia over dissents by Taft and Justice Holmes. Justice George Sutherland, one of the Harding appointees, wrote the majority opinion, proclaiming that "freedom of contract is...the general rule and restraint the exception." The legislation at issue could not be justified in his view because it "exacts from the employer an arbitrary payment for a purpose and upon a basis having no causal connection with his business, or the contract or the work the employee engages to do." This was because the minimum wages were established based upon the needs of the employee "to ensure her subsistence, health, and morals."

After *Adkins*, the Supreme Court continued to strike down both federal and state legislation which attempted to regulate business. Often using theories of freedom of contract or substantive due process, the Supreme Court struck down over 180 state laws of various types between 1899 and 1937.

Herbert Hoover: The Great Depression and
Early Efforts at Government Intervention in the
Economy.

The presidential administrations of Warren Harding and Calvin Coolidge saw a growth in the concentration and profitability of American business in the "Roaring Twenties," and the economy appeared to be sound. A harsher reality became apparent after President Herbert Hoover assumed the office in early 1929.

When President Coolidge laconically announced by hand-written notes to members of the press that he would not seek election to a second full presidential term, the Republican Party turned to Herbert Hoover as its nominee. Hoover had an extensive record of government service, having served, among other positions, as head of the Food Administration in World War I, and as Secretary of Commerce under Presidents Harding and Coolidge. Hoover is generally regarded by historians to have been one of the most qualified individuals ever to be elected president. He had an engineering degree from Stanford, and expertise in organization and efficiency. Hoover had applied these skills to make a fortune in mining operations, and retired at the age of 40, having become a millionaire before the outbreak of World War I. "The Great Engineer" then decided to pursue a life of service, which he saw as "a great spiritual force."

With Hoover's election, the Republican Party returned to the brand of Progressivism which characterized the presidencies of Theodore Roosevelt and William Howard Taft. In his book, *Principles of Mining* (1909), for example, Hoover had approved of collective bargaining, an eight-hour day, and mine safety legislation. Hoover applied his talents in organizational efficiencies to the federal government when he served as Secretary of Commerce. In that position, he strove to make it more responsive to its business constituency by such initiatives as conducting business surveys, publishing business statistics, and devising model housing codes. He also proposed wide-ranging reorganizations of cabinet departments and government agencies to rationalize their operations.

On business regulation, Hoover stated his core belief in 1931, late in his presidency: "The sole function of government is to bring about a condition of affairs favorable to the beneficial development of private enterprise." He therefore perpetuated his predecessors' cooperative approach to the business community. He believed, as the *New Republic* put it, that business should take the steering wheel and do the driving itself. In the continuing spirit of voluntarism, Hoover also favored business-created codes of fair practices as vehicles to bring Progressive structure and order to industry, and some 200 such codes were formulated in his presidential administration.

In the early days of his administration, Hoover was able to secure the passage of the Agricultural Marketing Act of 1929 to address the serious agricultural depression which followed World War I. This legislation sought to bring order to the agricultural marketplace through voluntary cooperation between government and agriculture. A Federal Farm Board was created, and was authorized to grant $500 million to agricultural cooperatives and stabilization corporations, conditioned on production quotas being accepted by farmers. To the extent that any surplus was nevertheless produced by farms, the stabilization corporation was authorized to purchase the overproduction. This attempt to bring order to the agricultural market largely failed, and resulted in losses to the federal government of some $345 million.

Within the first eight months of Hoover's presidency, the stock market crashed in October 1929. This market crash signaled the start of the Great Depression of the 1930s, but was not its cause. Multiple factors were at the root of the Depression, including a lack of diversification in an economy overly reliant on automobile production and construction; low consumer purchasing power, with production outstripping the demand; a destabilized banking industry; disappearance of a European market for American goods, particularly in agriculture; defaults on American war loans to the European allies; declining imports resulting from high tariffs; an unsound monetary policy implemented by the Federal Reserve, which raised, rather than lowered, interest rates; and an unwise tax policy under which a large tax increase was imposed in 1932.

Hoover's response in the early days of the Depression was once again to pursue voluntary cooperation with business to address the continuing economic crisis. As William Leuchtenburg has noted, "virtually all of the responsibility for the economic health of the nation was left with corporate directors." Thus, Hoover scheduled a White House Conference of Business; encouraged trade associations to adopt codes of fair practices; obtained pledges from business not to cut wages; sought to obtain non-strike pledges and withdrawals of wage increase requests from labor; sought pledges from utilities and railroads to expand construction; and, under his administration, the Federal Reserve eased credit, with the exception of credit extended to banks for broker loans. In 1930, in addition, the Hoover Administration obtained authorization for an expenditure of $150 million to fund the construction of new public buildings, in an attempt to revivify the important construction sector of the economy. By May of 1930, President Hoover was convinced that these initiatives had been successful, and he announced that "The Depression is over." Unfortunately, he was wrong, and the economy worsened in the last six months of 1930. The key automobile and steel industries declined, and some 1352 banks failed, 600 of which collapsed in November and December of that year. Banks responded by creating a liquidity crisis, calling loans and foreclosing on home loans, actions which only further depressed the housing market.

In 1931, an ongoing European depression made things worse, and Hoover agreed to a one-year moratorium on repayment of the Allied war debt in an effort to allow the European economy to recover. Ultimately, however, $1.5 billion in German and Austrian debt became worthless, and Hoover's actions were insufficient to stem the tide of domestic depression. The situation worsened further when Britain announced that it was abandoning the gold standard in September of 1931. Within 30 days of that decision, 522 more United States banks failed.

Hoover next attempted to revive the economy with a National Credit Corporation, under which banks voluntarily established a credit pool of $500 million to assist weaker banks. This effort soon failed after a few weeks, with only $10 million in loans being extended. By the end of 1931, some 2294 banks failed in that year, about

twice the number of the previous year. Hoover nevertheless continued to insist on voluntary efforts to address
the Depression, rejecting direct government grants to
the unemployed, which he denigrated as a "dole," and
called instead for voluntary organizations to assist the
poor and unemployed.

By 1932, Hoover recognized that his voluntaris-
tic approach had not worked, and he turned to direct
governmental regulation of the economy through the
Reconstruction Finance Corporation. Modeled on the
World War I experience of the War Finance Corporation,
the RFC was designed to prop up failing financial institutions. It had an initial funding of $500 million, to be
supplemented with an additional $1.5 billion, for emer-
gency loans to banks, insurance companies, railroads,
and agricultural stabilization corporations. Hoover also
secured passage of the Glass-Steagall Act of 1932 which
freed up $750 million in gold reserves for business use,
and expanded the collateral eligible to be pledged for
federal loans to businesses. Finally, in a watered-down
version of Hoover's proposal, the Federal Home Loan
Bank was permitted to accept mortgage paper as security for loans. Once again, with some initial improvement
in the economy, Hoover thought that his legislation had
ended the Depression. That was not to be the case, and
he was soundly trounced by Franklin D. Roosevelt in
the election of 1932, in which Hoover won less than 40
percent of the popular vote.

CHAPTER SIX
REGULATION WITH A VENGEANCE: FDR'S NEW DEALS

The election of Franklin Delano Roosevelt as president in 1932 not only brought about the end of Republican rule for the next 20 years, but also began a transformational change in the United States federal government. Reelected three times, Roosevelt expanded the role of the federal government in numerous areas, including in business regulation. His approach provided a stark contrast with the historical Republican approach predating Theodore Roosevelt and William Howard Taft, in which business took the lead, with minimal governmental supervision. With only limited exceptions, Franklin Roosevelt gave lip service to this "true concert of interests" approach. Instead, while campaigning in 1932, he declared that "I favor economic planning not for this period alone but for our needs for a long time to come." And that economic planning was intense and far-reaching.

The Supreme Court's decision in *Wickard v. Filburn* (1942) provides the extreme example of how far the Roosevelt Administration stretched the federal regulatory power over private business. That case presented the question as to the limits of federal power to regulate a farmer's production on his own farm for his own use. Roscoe Filburn violated the wheat quota established by Roosevelt's Agricultural Adjustment Act by growing wheat on 23 acres, rather than on the 11.1 acre limit set by the Act for the year in question. Although at least some of the additional wheat would be consumed by the Filburn family, the Supreme Court (eight of whose members had been appointed or elevated by President Roosevelt) unanimously decided that congressional power under the Interstate Commerce Clause permitted the federal government to prevent Filburn from growing wheat in excess of his allotment on his own farm for his own use. That this was a radical departure from the past is perhaps best illustrated by what Justice Edward White used as a reductio ad absurdam argument in his dissenting opinion in the *Northern Securities* case discussed in Chapter 4. There, White argued that a broad construction of the Sherman Act might lead to the implausible situation in which "if it were judged by Congress that the farmer in sowing his crops should be limited to a certain production because overproduction would give power to affect commerce, Congress could regulate that subject." White saw such a result as absurd because it would "destroy the state and Federal governments," and create in their place "a government endowed with the arbitrary power to disregard the great guaranty of life, liberty, and property and every other safeguard upon which organized civil society depends."

The First New Deal

The "New Deal" Roosevelt promised to the nation did not provide an organized or even coherent approach to business regulation. Instead, the spate of legislation which was enacted, especially in his first term, represented ad hoc, hoped-for solutions with no discernible economic rationale, an approach which Roy Jenkins has characterized as "a sort of stumbling Keynesianism." This scattered approach was deliberate on Roosevelt's part because he was committed to experimentation to resolve the drastic economic situation which confronted him. In his view, the proper approach was to "Take a method and try it. If it fails, admit it frankly and try another. But above all, try something."

In seeking to expand federal power over private business, Roosevelt skillfully employed a moralistic approach; he demonized selected businessmen, reprising his cousin Theodore Roosevelt's attack on "malefactors of great wealth." His first inaugural address reflected this approach, with biblical allusions which quoted the Old Testament and paraphrased the New Testament. He announced that "the rulers of the exchange of mankind's goods have failed, through their own stubbornness and their own incompetence, have admitted their failure, and abdicated. Practices of the unscrupulous money changers stand indicted in the court of public opinion, rejected by the hearts and minds of men.... Stripped of the lure of profit by which to induce our people to follow their false leadership, they have resorted to exhortations, pleading tearfully for restored confidence. They know only the rules of the generation of self-seekers. They have no vision, and where there is no vision the people perish. The money changers have fled from their high seats in the temple of our civilization. We may now restore that temple to the ancient truths. The measure of the restoration lies in the extent to which we apply social values more noble than mere monetary profit.... there must be an end to a conduct in banking and business which too often has given to a sacred trust the likeness of callous and selfish wrongdoing. Small wonder that confidence languishes, for it thrives only on honesty, on honor, on the sacredness of obligations, on faithful protection, on unselfish performance; without them it cannot live."

The enmity expressed towards the banking and business communities in Roosevelt's inaugural address continued throughout his presidency, and also embraced his political opponents. Roosevelt pursued these foes with vigor, particularly in his second term. But even in the first term, J.P. Morgan's son, who was the successor to the financial titan, was summoned before a congressional committee and forced publicly to admit he had (legally) paid no United States taxes from 1930 to 1932. Later, Roosevelt would prosecute both banker millionaire and former Treasury Secretary Andrew Mellon for tax evasion and utility magnate Samuel Insull for criminal fraud. Both were acquitted, but only after considerable negative publicity and high defense costs.

Banking and Currency Reform: Roosevelt's first term began with a blitz of legislation in what has become known as the "Hundred Days." He began with legislation aimed at the banking crisis, elevating the role of the federal government while diminishing the role of the "money changers" at whose feet the banking crisis had been laid in his inaugural address. On March 6, 1933, two days after his inauguration, Roosevelt ordered all banks in the United States closed for a "bank holiday." An Emergency Banking Act gave the federal government the power to inspect and to reorganize the banks which had survived while hundreds of others had failed during the Hoover Administration. Within three days, three out of four banks which were inspected reopened, and popular confidence in the soundness of the banking system was restored. Moreover, through the Reconstruction Finance Corporation begun under the Hoover Administration, the federal government provided additional capital to assure the solvency of weaker banks by purchasing over $1 billion of preferred stock in half of all the banks in the United States. The RFC head, Jesse Jones, sought to advance the federal government's control over the banking industry even further, telling the American Bankers Association that bankers should "take the government into partnership with you in providing...credit."

The Emergency Banking Act was followed by the Glass-Steagall Act of 1933, which was strengthened through amendments in 1935. This far-reaching legislation mandated the divorce of commercial banks, which engaged in lending, from investment banks, which engaged in securities transactions. The Act also authorized the government to stop speculative bank activities, and established the system of federal deposit insurance still in force today. (Curiously from today's perspective, the concept of deposit insurance was at first opposed by President Roosevelt, and the younger J.P. "Jack" Morgan called it "absurd.")

The federal government was also authorized to manage the monetary system more closely and to weaken the gold standard supporting the dollar. In one of his early "Fireside Chats" - radio addresses to the American people - Roosevelt candidly acknowledged that "we are... continuing to move toward a managed currency." In order to do this, the federal government was authorized to monetize silver and utilize greenbacks, with the gold backing the dollar ultimately set under the Gold Standard Act of 1934 at $35.02, which represented a devaluation of approximately 60 percent.

Agricultural Reform: The Roosevelt Administration next turned to the farming crisis in the Hundred Days' legislation. The agricultural sector of the economy faced serious and continuing problems, with farmers' income down some 50 percent in the prior four years. Twenty thousand farms were being foreclosed upon each month, and the prices of agricultural produce had declined 60 percent between 1926 and 1933. In the Agricultural Adjustment Act of 1933, the federal government addressed this crisis by effectively taking over the agricultural sector. As Roscoe Filburn would discover, agricultural production on farms was limited and farmers were paid not to grow seven key commodities, including wheat, corn, and cotton, with limitations also imposed on how many hogs were permitted by the federal government to be raised in order to control pork prices. In 1933 alone, $200 million was paid to farmers not to raise cotton, with some 10 million acres of cotton removed from production. Similarly, eight million acres of wheat were removed from production, and payments of $100 million were made to the farmers who acceded to the congressional mandate not to produce that commodity above the limits imposed. This radical intervention of the federal government into the lives and businesses of farmers rewarded the farming community in the short run by guaranteeing it higher prices for what was produced and restoring the sector to profitability. Both prices and farm income rose as a result of the Agricultural Adjustment Act. But the allotments also led to public outrage when some six million young pigs were killed to assure that hog production was kept within proper limits, and consumers in the throes of an ongoing Great Depression complained when farm prices, as planned, rose. As one consumer wrote, the slaughter of the young pigs "has raised pork prices until today we poor people cannot have a piece of bacon."

In the administration of the Agricultural Adjustment Act, the Roosevelt Administration relied for implementation on the American Farm Bureau Federation. This group, however, favored the interests of large producers at the expense of small farmers, including tenant farmers. Ultimately, the Supreme Court in 1936 declared the Agricultural Adjustment Act unconstitutional in *United States v. Butler*, striking down the tax which financed the payments to farmers as violative of the reserved rights of the states under the Tenth Amendment. The Act was rewritten to address the problem, and new legislation was passed in 1938.

The radical nature of the Agricultural Adjustment Act, judged by the history of the peacetime federal regulation which preceded it, is apparent. Through it, the federal government directly intruded into an important market, mandating a reduction in production of consumer commodities in order to raise prices. Had this been done by private parties, it would have been a per se violation of the Sherman Antitrust Act.

Business Regulation: In its initial attempt to regulate industrial enterprises, the Roosevelt Administration took a less intrusive approach than it pursued in the farming sector. In a May, 1933 Fireside Chat, President Roosevelt called for "a partnership in planning" with business, but noted that the federal government had the "right [to] prevent...unfair practices." The National Industrial Recovery Act which was enacted one month later was one area in which the government-business cooperative approach of the Hoover Administration was continued. Thus, the Act permitted major industries to get together with an exemption from the antitrust laws, which were suspended while the Act was in force, to establish "codes of fair competition" which regulated prices, established pricing floors, set production limits, protected collective bargaining rights, and imposed fair labor standards, including minimum wages, maximum 35 to 40 hour work weeks, and the prohibition of child labor. Violations of the Act were criminalized, with jail terms authorized to be imposed upon individuals.

The approach taken in the NIRA reflected the

Progressive ideal of fostering more efficient business organizations. Ultimately, some 22 million workers fell under some 700 codes of fair competition, but the administration fell under the control of large corporations, a control that led both to higher consumer prices and the disadvantaging of small competitors. In addition, the reduction of production which resulted from most of the codes of fair competition lowered wages, worsening the Great Depression. Two UCLA economists, Harold Cole and Lee Ohanian, calculated that the NIRA and other anti-competition and pro-labor laws and initiatives prolonged the Great Depression for seven years. This stemmed from the fact that, given the state of the economy, wages in certain industries attained levels 25 percent higher then they should have been, and prices roses to some 23 percent above the appropriate levels. Professor Ohanian observed that "High prices and high wages in an economic slump run contrary to everything we know about market forces in economic downturns."

The National Recovery Administration formed under the NIRA quickly foundered, and the Supreme Court put the agency (as well as the country) out of its misery when it declared the Act unconstitutional in the famous case of *Schechter Poultry Corporation v. United States* (1935). There, the court found that the NIRA exceeded the limits of congressional power to regulate commerce under the Interstate Commerce Clause, and also unlawfully delegated legislative power to the president, conferring "unfettered discretion to make whatever laws he thinks may be needed or advisable for the rehabilitation and expansion of trade or industry." In a concurring opinion, Justice Benjamin Cardozo saw the NIRA as "delegation running riot."

One extremely significant part of the NIRA which survived was the Public Works Administration, which provided massive funding for construction projects to revive that key sector of the economy. Originally authorized to spend $3.3 billion, the Public Works Administration ultimately spent some $6 billion between 1933 and 1939 in the largest public works program ever implemented to that time. The results of the PWA can still be seen today across the country. Some of the more notable projects it financed were the Boulder Dam, the Triborough Bridge in New York, and even the electrification of the Pennsylvania Railroad line between Washington D.C. and New York City.

A much more intrusive federal system of regulation was imposed upon the securities industry initially in the Securities Act of 1933, and later in the Securities Exchange Act of 1934. Over bitter and prolonged opposition from Wall Street, this legislation sought to make the securities markets transparent and stripped of manipulative practices. The 1933 Act mandated disclosure of critical financial information to protect buyers of securities, and to end trading based upon inside information available only to bankers and management. As President Roosevelt put it in 1933, the Act placed upon the seller "the burden of telling the whole truth." The 1934 Act went even further, regulating the stock exchanges by prohibiting misrepresentations in the purchase and sale of securities as well as certain manipulative practices. The Act also established margin requirements, curtailing the ability to make speculative purchases without the buyer committing significant financial resources. The New York investment community, led by Richard Whitney, the president of the New York Stock Exchange, and the partners of what Ron Chernow has termed the "House of Morgan," bitterly opposed enactment of the 1934 legislation, warning that it would turn Wall Street into "a deserted village" and destroy the capital markets. Despite their protestations, the bill was enacted and with the passage of this securities legislation, the investment community forever lost the right to self-regulate. In its stead, the federal government stepped in as monitor and supervisor of the securities industry, a result once considered unthinkable, at least by the investment community.

Electric Power Production: In another intrusion into the private marketplace, and in contrast to the co-operative approach of the NIRA, the Tennessee Valley Authority provided direct government competition to private electric utilities. The underlying legislative intent was to increase the use of electricity and to lower the prices charged for it. The TVA constructed dams in seven states to control flooding on the Tennessee River while also generating electricity for the Tennessee Valley and fostering the economic development of the region. Government-established electricity pricing was to serve as a yardstick to evaluate and ultimately to reduce the charges from private electric utilities. The strategy worked; the TVA was able to produce electric power at about half the cost of private companies, and electricity rates fell. The government had now emerged as a competitor to private industry.

Housing Regulation: In 1934, the federal government turned to regulation of the housing market by enacting the National Housing Act. That legislation established the Federal Housing Authority, which was empowered to insure private mortgages and to establish mortgage interest rates. Once again, the underlying purpose, as with the Tennessee River Authority and the Agricultural Adjustment Act, was to expand and/or stabilize a market. In addition, the federal government continued to enter private markets and to set the rules under which private businesses could function in those markets. As such, the time for unregulated competition had ended in many major sectors of the economy, including banking, agriculture, securities, construction, public utilities, and housing.

The Second New Deal

The flurry of legislation which began in the Hundred Days and extended into 1934 comprised the legacy of the First New Deal. As President Roosevelt entered 1935, he faced vigorous opposition to his inconsistent approaches to banking, business, and agriculture from both the right and the left. Roosevelt therefore pivoted to meet the more significant challenges to his Administration from the left, beginning what would become known as the Second New Deal.

Attack From The Left: While Roosevelt was confronted with multiple challengers from the left, the

two most significant were Senator Huey P. Long of
Louisiana and the Michigan "Radio Priest," Father
Charles Coughlin. Long, who served as both Governor
of Louisiana and as a United States Senator, was a serious political threat to Roosevelt, and was expected to
be a third party candidate against him in 1936. Long
championed the common man and entitled his 1930 bi-
ography *Every Man A King*. He concentrated his campaign around a "Share the Wealth Plan," a proposal
which was meant to combat the power of concentrated
wealth. Long estimated that four percent of the population, including "Morgan and Rockefeller and Mellon
and Baruch," controlled 85 percent of the wealth. Long
wanted that wealth redistributed so that all the people
in the United States would receive a $5000 distribution
for a "household estate" and a guaranteed annual wage
of $2500. In addition, all incomes would be limited to
$8 million, which Long soon reduced to $1 million.
Inheritances would be capped at $5 million; workers
would receive pensions; and all Americans would be
entitled to a free college education. "Share the Wealth"
clubs sprang up across the nation with membership estimated as high as nine million people. Long's meteoric
political rise and lavish but popular spending on public
improvements in Louisiana ended only with his assassination in September of 1935.

Father Charles Coughlin, the "Radio Priest" from
Michigan, had a much more sophisticated economic
program than Long. His proposals were rooted in the
papal social justice encyclicals of Pope Leo XIII and
his successors, with a heavy dose of Populism stirred

in. Coughlin's radio program, "The Golden Hour of the Little Flower," had an audience of 40 million, and required Coughlin to maintain a staff of four secretaries and 106 clerks to answer his massive mail, which exceeded that received by President Roosevelt. Coughlin's platform included the following: monetary inflation through the use of silver and paper money as currency; nationalization of all banks; abolition of the Federal Reserve System; establishment of a national welfare system; and state control of the economy, including state management of finance capitalism. Coughlin at first supported Roosevelt, proclaiming that "the New Deal is Christ's Deal," but later began his own political organization, and was expected to support Long's third-party candidacy in 1936.

In order to combat this attack from the left, Roosevelt sought to undercut the proposals of Long and Coughlin with those of his own, mirroring them in several instances. Roosevelt's strategy included three principal initiatives - relief legislation, tax increases, and additional business regulation.

Relief Legislation: Roosevelt first obtained legislative approval of measures designed to provide relief to the elderly, the unemployed, the disabled, and children. Principal among these was the 1935 Social Security Act. That legislation established a system under which the elderly who had been employed would receive monthly payments financed by contributions made during the time that they worked by their employer and by themselves. In addition, unemployed individuals would receive payments under a system of insurance funded by employers. Finally, disabled individuals and dependent children would be granted financial assistance.

A second major relief effort came through the Emergency Relief Act of 1935. Roosevelt established the Works Progress Administration, which supplemented and greatly expanded the work of the Public Works Administration discussed above. The WPA employed some 8.5 million people in the eight years after its establishment, and spent $11 billion during that time. Its projects significantly alleviated the unemployment problem. In 1936 alone, for example, the agency was responsible for providing work for seven percent of all American workers. The WPA financed the construction of 100,000 bridges; about the same number of public buildings; 500,000 miles of highway; 8000 public parks; and 600 airports.

Tax Legislation: Roosevelt's next major initiative in his Second New Deal was a system of progressive taxation designed to meet Long's clamor to "soak the rich." In the Revenue Act of 1935, the Roosevelt Administration raised taxes on personal and corporate income, as well as on inheritances. In justifying high inheritance taxes, Roosevelt declared that "The transmission of wealth from generation to generation of vast fortunes...is not consistent with the ideas and sentiments of the American people." On the high tax rates imposed on the wealthy, the president told a reporter at the time that "It might be necessary to throw to the wolves" the 46 people making over $1 million a year. In fact, the Revenue Act did little to alleviate the nation's financial crisis, and contained some provisions which were simply symbolic, including a 79 percent tax rate on personal incomes over $5 million, which applied only to one person, John D. Rockefeller.

Roosevelt reveled in the vitriolic opposition his tax and other Second New Deal legislation generated among the wealthy. He characterized his approach as constituting an attack on the "great accumulations of wealth," and on "the forces of selfishness and lust for power." With great pride, he told the Congress in his 1936 State of the Union Message that "We have earned the hatred of entrenched greed."

Business Regulation: The third prong of the Second New Deal – and the one most significant for our focus – was directed to the regulation of industry. The three most significant pieces of legislation which were enacted dealt with industry's obligation to recognize the rights of labor; federal control over public utilities; and additional regulation of banking.

With the passage of the National Labor Relations Act, popularly known as the Wagner Act, the federal government swung from a cooperative approach with business to a strong proponent of labor, empowering unions to organize backed by the support of government enforcement mechanisms. The Wagner Act mandated collective bargaining; barred labor injunctions; and prohibited company unions. Significantly, it also established a new agency, the National Labor Relations Board, investing it with a wide range of powers to ban unfair labor practices, to issue cease and desist orders, and to compel recognition of unions by business. The Board was extremely active; one measure of that activity is reflected in its employment of lawyers. The original complement of 14 lawyers in 1935 grew exponentially to 226 attorneys by 1939.

Despite vigorous industry opposition, including a court suit to declare the Wagner Act unconstitutional, the Act was upheld by the Supreme Court in *National Labor Relations Board v. Jones & Laughlin Steel Corp.* (1937). While four dissenting justices complained that upholding the Act under the Commerce Clause departed from "well-established principles," including those just recently reaffirmed in the *Schechter* decision, Chief Justice Hughes' majority opinion found that Congress had the power to regulate activities, even of an intrastate character, "if they have such a close and substantial relation to interstate commerce that their control is essential or appropriate to protect that commerce from burdens and obstructions." As such, the federal government had the power to reach into and to regulate employment affairs even at a local steel plant. The different approach taken in the *Jones & Laughlin* opinion to the Commerce Clause was somewhat foreshadowed by the decision in *West Coast Hotel v. Parrish* (1937), which explicitly overruled the freedom of contract holding of *Adkins v. Children's Hospital*, a decision which was discussed in the previous chapter. *Jones & Laughlin* ruled that the holding in *Adkins* was a "departure from the true application of the principles governing the regulation by the state of the relation of employer and employed."

Jones & Laughlin represented only the beginning of the Supreme Court's more capacious view of the Commerce Clause; by the time Roscoe Filburn took his case to the Supreme Court, congressional power under the Commerce Clause was viewed even more broadly.

A second piece of legislation regulating business, the Public Utilities Holding Company Act of 1935, was aimed at the politically potent electric utility conglomerates in an attempt to weaken their power, and to strengthen the efforts of the Tennessee Valley Authority to provide cheap electricity. The Act was part of an overall plan to rein in political opponents such as Wendell Willkie, the head of the powerful Commonwealth and Southern Utility System, who would oppose Roosevelt as the Republican presidential candidate in 1940. Roosevelt also sought to demonize utility executives by such methods as the unsuccessful criminal fraud prosecution of Chicago utility executive Samuel Insull.

The Public Utilities Holding Company Act permitted the government to regulate the largest holding companies which effectively controlled the market for electricity. It required utility holding companies to limit their operations to one state, or to one integrated system, and subjected them to regulation by the Securities and Exchange Commission and the Federal Power Commission. Under the Act, the government was empowered to order the disbanding of holding companies which were in violation of these standards, and it successfully ordered the divesting of some $12 billion in holding company assets by 1948. The legislation also required public utility holding companies to obtain SEC approval to engage in any non-utility business, and to keep any such businesses separate from their utility operations.

The Banking Act of 1935 was the third major law regulating business in this period. It was enacted to strengthen the scheme of banking regulation established by the 1933 Glass-Steagall Act, and to combat the perception that the regional banks in the Federal Reserve system, particularly that in New York, continued to control monetary policy. While Father Coughlin and his followers sought to nationalize the banking system, the Banking Act rejected this approach but nodded to Coughlin by centralizing federal power over banking in Washington. Thus, the Act reorganized the Federal Reserve System so as to place power over monetary policy in Washington D.C., and to confer greater power over banking matters on the Secretary of the Treasury. The Federal Reserve Board was also given the power to purchase and sell government securities in open-market transactions to permit it, rather than the individual regional banks, to exercise monetary control.

Roosevelt's Second New Deal was an electoral elixir for both him and the Democratic Party. In the 1936 election, Roosevelt beat Governor Alf Landon, a Republican Progressive from Kansas, winning nearly 61 percent of the popular vote. Landon even lost his own state, carrying only Maine and Vermont. His percentage of the popular vote was a mere 36.5 percent. Coughlin's candidate, congressman William Lemke of North Dakota, took less than two percent of the popular vote. Significantly, Democrats won majorities in excess of 75 percent in both the United States Senate and the House of Representatives. The Second New Deal had prevailed.

The End of the New Deals

In his second inaugural address, President Roosevelt declared that "I see one-third of the nation ill-housed, ill-clad, ill-nourished." To combat this and other economic and social problems, he invoked his characterization of the vision of the Founders and called for a "strong government," which was necessary "to solve problems utterly beyond individual or local solution." In his view, "By using the new materials of social justice, we have undertaken to erect on the old foundations a more enduring structure for the better use of future generations."

Roosevelt's hope to build that "more enduring structure" would only be partially realized because the New Deal soon came to a grinding halt as a result of three factors. These were Roosevelt's plan to "pack" the Supreme Court with more malleable justices; his campaign to unseat conservative Democratic senators; and the "Roosevelt Recession" of 1937-1938.

Soon after his inauguration, and without prior notice, Roosevelt sent a Special Message to Congress on February 5, 1937, requesting legislation to permit him to appoint one new justice of the Supreme Court for every justice who was over 70 years old, up to a total of six new justices. The figure of six was not randomly chosen, since that was the number of justices who then were 70 or older. Roosevelt attacked the Supreme Court in a Fireside Chat, complaining that it was not pulling together in a united effort with the executive and legislative branches. His attack on the court stemmed from its decisions declaring unconstitutional much of the initial Hundred Days' legislation, and his fear that the legislation enacted in the Second New Deal, including the Social Security Act and the Wagner Act, would meet the same fate. Roosevelt's view of the court seemed to recapitulate the Populists' view of the justices as "tools and vassals... of the great corporations." In addition, he charged that older judges were only responsive to "the needs of another generation." This attempt to pack the court met with widespread opposition, and ultimately was defeated in the Senate by an overwhelming vote of 70 to 20. That result was greatly facilitated by a turnabout in the Supreme Court, which, as noted above, first upheld a Washington state minimum wage law in the case of *West Coast Hotel v. Parrish* (1937), and then, more importantly, upheld both the Social Security Act in two separate cases and the Wagner Act in *NLRB v. Jones & Laughlin Corp.* (1937). Moreover, Roosevelt ultimately was able to replace seven of the older justices through resignations and deaths, and to elevate an eighth, Harlan Stone, to Chief Justice.

A second development which slowed the legislative initiatives of what Roosevelt hoped to become a Third New Deal was Roosevelt's politically ill-advised campaign to unseat conservative, mainly southern, Democratic senators. Roosevelt badly miscalculated on this, failing to recognize that there was substantial resistance to the liberal, city-oriented programs of the New Deal not only in the South, but also in the rural sections of the nation in the West, Midwest, and even in New England. Outside of the cities, conservative

Democrats as well as Republicans were concerned with labor strikes, welfare payments, and the requirements to pay minimum wages. While Roosevelt devoted Fireside Chats in June and November 1938 to oppose the conservative Southern senators and to support their liberal challengers, he went down to a crushing defeat. Even some of the liberal Democratic incumbents, including the governors of Michigan and Pennsylvania, were defeated, and the Republican Party doubled its representation in the House of Representatives,and won an additional eight Senate seats in the off-year election of 1938.

The third significant development which stopped the Third New Deal in its infancy was what became known as "the Roosevelt Recession" of 1937-1938. Starting in August 1937, this recession resulted in a decline of 4.5 percent in the domestic Gross National Product, and an increase in unemployment from 14.3 percent in 1937 to 19 percent in 1938. Indeed, some two million workers were laid off during that period.

Against the background of these negative developments, there were only two tangible results of the Third New Deal. The sole significant new legislative accomplishment was enactment of the Fair Labor Standards Act in 1938. This legislation made mandatory several of the initiatives implemented under the codes of fair competition of the NRA, including a maximum workweek of 40 hours and the prohibition of child labor. In addition, a minimum hourly wage was established for most businesses, with exemptions for agricultural workers and workers in certain service industries. A new Agricultural Adjustment Act was also passed to overcome the constitutional problem which had led the Supreme Court to strike the previous version down in the *Butler* case.

The second significant impact of the Third New Deal on American industry was a full-throated assault by the Roosevelt Administration on "monopoly power." The one early cooperative stance with industry with the antitrust exemptions afforded under the NIRA was replaced by a reinvigorated antitrust enforcement policy. Under Thurman Arnold, the newly appointed head of the Department of Justice Antitrust Division, a flurry of antitrust suits ensued, and the legal staff of the Antitrust Division increased exponentially, such that it numbered almost 300 under Arnold's leadership.

With these limited results, the Third New Deal collapsed.

The Rise of the Administrative State

One of the lasting impacts of the Roosevelt presidencies on business emanates from the proliferation of administrative agencies it instituted. A regulatory state emerged with its mandates implemented (and often created) by multiple agencies, boards, and other entities, including the Agricultural Adjustment Administration, the Civil Aeronautics Board, the Federal Communications Commission, the Federal Deposit Insurance Corporation, the Federal Housing Administration, the National Labor Relations Board, and the Securities and Exchange Commission, as well as a multiplicity of other entities put together to manage the war effort of World War II. Moreover, other preexisting agencies such as the Federal

Power Commission had their mandates and powers expanded. Thus, under the various laws enacted as parts of the New Deals, business was subjected to ongoing regulation in many of its sectors, including agriculture, aviation, banking, communications, electric power, housing, labor relations, and securities transactions.

The continuing reliance by Congress today on administrative agencies to implement broad legislative directives by specific regulations drafted and implemented by this "fourth branch" of government subjects business to regulation which is both intensive and often unpredictable. Permitting administrative agencies to implement, and often to formulate, regulatory policy presents the problem of a potential for unconstitutional delegation of congressional power. This was the problem with the NIRA which the Supreme Court identified in its *Schechter* opinions. As such, the persistency of legislative grants of authority to administrative agencies to formulate regulations outlining precise parameters for business operations represents one of the most significant legacies of the "Roosevelt Revolution" for today's business person. This "fourth branch" of government still mandates exact parameters for business operations to this day, reversing the historical Republican approach of limiting regulation and permitting business to operate with minimal restraints.

CHAPTER SEVEN

THE MILITARY-INDUSTRIAL COMPLEX: WORLD WAR II, THE COLD WAR, AND AMERICAN BUSINESS

World War II

World War II, like World War I, fueled the growth of American business. Indeed, as Thomas Mc-Craw has noted, "In its effect on American business, World War II was the most significant event of the twentieth century." Business prospered from World War II primarily through implementing the call of President Franklin D. Roosevelt in his Fireside Chat of December 24, 1940, to become "the great arsenal of democracy."

Wars, including World War II, assist business in at least three distinct ways. First, wars create new markets, and new markets in turn generate industrial expansion. Second, wars also catalyze technological innovation and efficiency, making businesses more competitive. Third, wars also expand employment opportunities, and thus provide additional wages and salaries enabling more people to purchase the products produced by business. All of these aspects can be seen in the interaction of business and government in World War II.

How Business Became the Arsenal of Democracy

President Roosevelt served as the Assistant Secretary of the Navy under President Wilson in World War I. From first-hand experience, he observed that businesses had dominated the war effort and realized large profits from it. As such, he was determined to prevent business from taking over the war effort in World War II. His desire in this regard was made even more imperative by a flood of revisionist books opposing American entry into World War II by contending that World War I was instigated by arms merchants and Wall Street. Despite Roosevelt's preference to curb the power of big business, large corporations once again dominated the war production effort in World War II. "Dollar-a-year men" worked for the government on the war effort while staying on corporate payrolls. The government needed their assistance in order to generate the necessary production of war materials, diverting private industry's productive capacity from consumer goods. In order to obtain that assistance, Roosevelt's Secretary of War, Henry Stimson, realized that "If you are going to try to go to war, or to prepare for war, in a capitalist country, you have got to let business make money out of the process or business won't work."

As was the case in World War I, it was big business that profited most heavily from World War II. Only

large corporations were able to satisfy the huge requirements of the American war machine. As one Army general put it, "All the small plants of the country could
not turn out one day's requirement of ammunition." As
such, under the Controlled Materials Plan devised by
Ferdinand Eberstadt, a Wall Street investment banker
who served as vice chair of the War Production Board,
the largest group of prime contractors who supplied the
war effort was comprised of America's biggest corporations. Thus, 100 companies received two-thirds of all
military contracts awarded in World War II, while 30
percent of those contracts went to 10 companies. Those
10 companies included the "Big Three" automakers,
Bethlehem Steel, General Electric and several large
aircraft manufacturers, including Douglas, United, and
Lockheed. Other companies, such as IBM, also fueled
their growth through defense contracts awarded to them
in World War II.

In order to obtain the assistance of these large corporations to divert their productive capacity to the war effort, it was necessary for the Roosevelt Administration to
tamp down its hostility to business, and it did so. During
the preparation for and waging of World War II, corporations were given tax breaks, loans at favorable interest rates from the Reconstruction Finance Corporation,
and cost-plus contracts which generated large profits. In
addition, the ramped-up antitrust prosecutorial efforts
of the Third New Deal were shut down. This greater
governmental deference to business resulted in business
devoting one-half of its productive capacity to the war
effort by 1944.

World War II was also responsible for increasing corporate payrolls, plant, and equipment, and for creating industrial behemoths. For example, in 1939, some 26 percent of all American companies employed fewer than 100 workers. By 1945, that percentage had fallen to 19 percent. More significantly, when the war concluded, the large production facilities built with government assistance were sold at greatly discounted prices to large corporations. Two-thirds of those facilities, with a total value of $17 billion, were sold to only 78 companies.

How Business Won World War II and Obtained New Markets

The American economy expanded exponentially during World War II. The total costs of that war are estimated at $300 billion. That cost was ten times that of World War I, and represented twice the total expenditures of the federal government in the prior 150 years of its existence. The federal budget grew by a factor of 18 times, from expenditures of $9 billion in 1939 to expenditures of $166 billion in 1945. The federal debt, which was kept down by increased income taxes, still grew by a factor of five, from $49 billion in 1941 to $259 billion in 1945. The American Gross National Product grew two and one-half times between 1939 and 1945. The increased federal spending which resulted from the war effort represented a bonanza to business while also solving the immense unemployment problem which characterized the Great Depression. As late as 1940, 15 percent of the American workforce was unemployed. As a result of the war effort, unemployment dropped to approximately one percent by 1944 and the percentage of women in the workforce more than doubled. Some 10,500,000 workers were newly employed during the 1940s, while 16 million more served in the armed forces.

This huge war spending yielded a rich harvest in war machinery. During World War II, American business built or manufactured approximately 300,000 planes; 102,000 tanks; 88,000 ships, including 147 aircraft carriers; 2.3 million trucks; 6.5 million rifles; 635,000 jeeps; and 40 billion bullets. Production on this scale was made possible through the diversion of the industrial capacity of American business to the war effort. Auto manufacturers, for example, shifted their efforts from producing cars to producing tanks, jeeps, other military vehicles, and even aircraft engines. In addition, the key construction industry prospered through the building of multiple new facilities to support the war effort, including the 600,000 square-foot Pentagon building

Significantly, production of military equipment was not limited to the needs of the American armed forces alone. New markets were created for American business through supplying the needs of American allies in the war effort. Planes, ships, and other military equipment were produced for Britain, Russia and other Allied nations. Some $50 billion of aid was supplied to Allies, including $10 billion to Russia alone. 37,000 tanks, 43,000 planes, 800,000 trucks, and 2 million rifles were produced by American industry and supplied to our allies in World War II.

How World War II Catalyzed Technological Development

World War II generated an immense technological revolution which Thomas McCraw has characterized as a Third Industrial Revolution rooted in scientific research. There were two principal manifestations of this revolution. McCraw focused upon the generation of new products and technologies. These included such items as the development of computers; advances in electronics and telecommunications; creation of synthetics of all types, including synthetic rubber which was vital for the war effort and otherwise unavailable domestically; and the creation of new drugs and medical equipment, as well as the development of more obviously war-related products such as microwave and air-to-surface-vessel radar and rockets. The Office of Scientific Research and Development, created in 1941 and headed by Vannevar Bush of the Massachusetts Institute of Technology, facilitated these innovations, expending some $100 million on research and development, and creating a partnership with American universities.

The most momentous scientific development of World War II was the atomic bomb, which was initially tested on July 16, 1945, with the two bombs produced being dropped on Hiroshima and Nagasaki, Japan, three weeks later. The technology for producing the atomic bomb came mainly from scientists who had fled from Germany, Hungary, and Italy, including Enrico Fermi, the Nobel Prize winner for Physics in 1938. Fermi relocated to the University of Chicago as an enemy alien from Italy, and directed the efforts which led to the first chain reaction in December 1942. In addition to Fermi and several noted Hungarian scientists, including Leo Szilard, Hitler's rejection of what he termed "Jewish physics" prevented Germany from obtaining the atomic bomb, and helped to populate the United States scientific establishment with several leading German Jewish scientists.

The development of the atomic bomb was led by two people, the scientist Robert Oppenheimer and General Leslie Groves. Together they headed the Manhattan Project, which was instituted in September of 1942. Headquartered in secrecy in Los Alamos, New Mexico, the Manhattan Project employed between 125,000 and 150,000 individuals at a cost of some $2 billion. The renowned scientist Niels Bohr later observed that "I told you it couldn't be done without turning the whole country into a factory. You have just done that."

In addition to the development of new technologies and products, American industry also became highly efficient in producing products for the war effort. Two notable examples are found in the production of ships and airplanes. Under the leadership of Henry J. Kaiser, whose previous accomplishments included building the world's largest cement plant and the first integrated steel mill, "Liberty Ships" were constructed in several locations, including California. Using the American System of manufacture, which employed prefabrication and interchangeable parts, Kaiser was able to shorten the time for building a ship from 105 days in 1942 to 41 days in 1943 and, by the end of the war, to 17 days. Similar operations by other corporations were devoted to producing airplanes for the allies. The most significant operation was the Ford Motor Willow Creek, Michigan plant which employed the American System to build B-24 bombers. These planes flew longer and higher than the comparable German planes and had better navigation and radar systems. Significantly, while the American System of manufacture was able to ultimately produce a B-24 at Willow Creek in 63 minutes, using prefabricated parts, German airplanes were produced individually, with more precision, but with far less total output.

World War II and the subsequent Cold War revived and invigorated the American business economy in the ways set forth above. What was the result? As Paul Johnson put it, World War II "acted as an immense bull market, encouraging American entrepreneurial skills to fling the country's seemingly inexhaustible resources of materials and manpower into a bottomless pool of consumption."

The Post-War Economic Boom

The economist Daniel Yankelovich has described the period from 1945 to 1970 as a "quarter century of sustained growth at the highest rates in recorded history." In that period, the Gross National Product grew from $200 billion to $500 billion. By the end of the 1940s, the United States was responsible for 50 percent of the world's manufacturing and generated 42 percent of world income. In the decade of the 1950s, the American economy expanded even further, with

GNP increasing by a factor of some 37 percent in that decade alone.

Much of this growth was fueled by government spending at both the federal and state government levels. The growth in federal spending had risen from $9.4 billion in 1939 to $95.2 billion in 1945, the final year of World War II. While federal spending declined immediately after the war ended, it began growing again before the end of the decade, reaching some $43.1 billion by 1950. State and local spending doubled to $21.3 billion in 1948, with much of the spending devoted to the construction of schools and the building of roads. Thomas McCraw points to a "three-way alliance of government, higher education, and business [which]...emerged during World War II [and] now became entrenched."

Business was a prime beneficiary of this government spending. Much of that spending was directed toward industrial research and development. One measure of this growth came in the number of engineers who were employed. That number increased from about 50,000 engineers in 1946 to approximately 300,000 in 1961.

Federal dollars were particularly important in supporting research and development in the electronics industry, financing some 70 percent of R&D expenditures in that sector of the economy. In turn, this research and development undertaking gave rise to a rapid growth in the development of new products including transistors, which were used in radios, hearing aids and computers. Increased spending on research and development also gave rise to a burgeoning industry in computers.

Significantly, the industrial development of computers was rooted in defense requirements. IBM, for example, reached its Cold War dominance in computers based upon defense contracts. Indeed, in the year 1950 alone, the federal government financed some 15,000 research projects in private industry for the military.

Research and development also spurred the growth of a rapidly expanding pharmaceutical drug industry. That industry, in turn, developed important new medical advances, including the 1955 Salk vaccine against polio, as well as new product lines which offered multiple wonder drugs. American industries also developed novel products for consumers, including frozen foods, garbage disposals, electric dryers, nylon stockings, and vinyl coverings.

Industry returned to producing consumer products to satisfy a pent-up demand resulting from the diversion of corporate energies from the consumer market to war needs during World War II. The automobile industry was a major beneficiary of this pent-up demand, and General Motors in 1955 became the first United States corporation to reach $1 billion in sales. Consumers also bought furniture, clothing, jewelry, and televisions once war restrictions on industrial production were lifted.

Postwar developments also led to a geographic dispersal of the American population to expanding suburban communities in the 1950s. This expansion benefited construction projects in particular, with the building of new housing communities, including "Levittowns" in Long Island, Pennsylvania, and New Jersey, as well as suburban shopping centers; gas stations; hotels; motels, such as the Holiday Inn chain; restaurants, including McDonalds; and drive-in theaters. Once again, the federal government was instrumental in assisting business growth in this area in several ways. First, the Interstate Highway Act of 1956 subsidized the building of more than 40,000 miles of interstate highways, initially based upon a military justification, but which in fact worked to facilitate suburban expansion and construction. Second, the Federal Housing Administration financed ownership of much of the new homes which were built in this formative period.

The absence of a war mentality coupled with a return to prosperity also led to the largest increase in American population ever during the decade of the 1950s. This "Baby Boom" expanded business markets even further, with both old and new children's products manufactured in increasing quantities. The postwar economy also witnessed increased consumer spending financed with an 800 percent increase in consumer credit from 1945 through 1957, fueled by a new credit card industry.

Given this increased prosperity, American labor responded with multiple strikes seeking higher wages. The period witnessed nearly 5000 work stoppages involving more than 4.5 million workers. The resulting disruption of industrial production led to enactment of the Taft-Hartley Act of 1947 which cut back on the protections granted to labor under the Roosevelt Administration's Wagner Act. Taft-Hartley reacted to a perceived over-reaching by unions by banning secondary boycotts and union shops, permitting states to outlaw union shops under so-called "right to work" laws. The legislation also mandated 80 day cooling off periods for strikes deemed to affect the national interest.

The Marshall Plan

In addition to benefiting from a post-war domestic economic boom, American business growth was also accelerated through sales made to Europe under the Economic Recovery Program, popularly known as the Marshall Plan. This initiative, announced in 1947, has been described by Bruce Kuklick as "the most extraordinary collaboration of businessmen and government."

The Marshall Plan was designed to assist the economic recovery of World War II allies of United States in Western Europe, but it also significantly aided American industry. Businessmen recognized that the Marshall Plan would assist the further growth of American business in foreign markets, and collaborated with government in a joint effort: the government provided the money, while the Economic Recovery Program was run by private businessmen. The ERP chair was Paul Hoffman, the former President of the Studebaker car company, who led the organization until 1950.

Between 1948 and 1952, the United States poured over $13 billion in aid into Western Europe under the Plan, much of which was utilized by the European countries to purchase products manufactured in America to assist in the rebuilding of infrastructure and the erection of modern factories, steel mills, hydroelectric plants, and manufacturing facilities. United States industries, particularly those manufacturing capital goods, machinery, steel, and electrical products, as well as the agricultural and defense industries, were prime beneficiaries of this American post-war aid to Europe.

European politicians appreciated the assistance that the American financial aid afforded in rebuilding their economies, but they also feared an increased American presence in, and potential domination over, those economies. One British politician characterized the Marshall Plan as the start of "the Yankee businessman's invasion of Europe." The French politician and journalist, Jean-Jacques Servan-Schreiber, similarly felt that American investments "do not so much involve a transfer of capital, as the actual *seizure of power* within the European economy." These observations were not without merit. As Charles Mee has documented, direct investments by American businesses into British and European industries "took off... immediately after the war," particularly in mining, manufacturing and petroleum, and companies controlled by American businesses were responsible by the 1960s for a majority of the production in the United Kingdom of such items as shoe machinery, sewing machines, typewriters, calculating machines, breakfast cereals, automobiles, pharmaceutical drugs, petroleum-refining construction equipment, tractors, vacuum cleaners, and a host of other products. The Marshall Plan was thus both a great American humanitarian endeavor and a significant boon to American business.

The Expansion of the Defense Industry

James Patterson reports that a common saying during the postwar period was that "The hand that signs the work contract is the hand that shapes the future." Defense spending, as noted above, did in fact shape the American economy during and after World War II, both domestically and internationally. As a share of Gross Domestic Product, defense spending rose from 5 percent in 1952 to more than 14 percent in 1953. In 1953, defense spending topped $50 billion, and it ranged between $40 and $46 billion for the rest of that decade. As a percentage of the federal budget, defense spending was even more significant. In 1949, it accounted for approximately 1/3 of the federal budget; in the 1950s, that percentage grew to approximately 50 percent, leading some commentators to describe this as "military Keynesianism."

There were four principal factors which led to this dramatic increase in defense spending. First, the Cold War gave rise to an increasing American concern regarding Russian expansion and aggression, beginning shortly after the end of World War II. The diplomat George Kennan was influential in developing the theory of "containment" of the Soviet Union in his "Long Telegram" of 1946 and in his article, "The Sources of Soviet Conduct," written anonymously as "X" and published in *Foreign Affairs* in 1947. Kennan's theory helped to shape and secure approval for the Marshall Plan. It also contributed to a military push to increase defense spending, which increased even more with the outbreak of the Korean War in 1950, and the issuance of NSC-68 in the same year. Indeed, the 1950 defense expenditure of $13 billion increased nearly four-fold to $50.4 billion in 1953, with an aim not only to contain, but also to achieve superior power vis-a-vis Soviet Russia. The Cold War itself led Secretary of Defense Charles Wilson, who formerly had headed General Motors, to refer to a "permanent war economy."

A second factor which increased defense spending was the development of the hydrogen bomb in 1952, with an attendant perceived need to produce rockets and missiles capable of delivering such bombs as far away as Russia. Yet a third contributing factor was the reaction to the Russian launch of the Sputnik satellite in 1957, which reinforced the recommendations for increased military spending that had been made in the Gaither Report of the same year. That Report led to calls for increased military spending of $44 billion over the next five years. The spending which resulted included development of a U.S. Space Program and the establishment of the National Aeronautics and Space Administration in 1958.

A fourth major factor which increased military spending was the fear of a "missile gap" with Russia which became a political hot button in the period 1958 to 1960. This fear became a major campaign theme in the successful presidential campaign of John F. Kennedy in 1960.

President Eisenhower's Farewell Address: Warnings of Emerging Threats From the "Military-Industrial Complex" and the Technological Revolution

General Dwight D. Eisenhower was the most notable war hero of World War II. Based on his popularity, Eisenhower was elected president in 1952, serving two terms which ended in early 1961. Despite his military background, Eisenhower worried about the effects on America and its people from the greatly increased military spending during his presidency. In 1953, for example, he observed that "Every gun that is made, every warship launched, every rocket fired signifies, in the final sense, a theft from those who hunger and are not fed, those who are cold and not clothed."

Even more significantly, Eisenhower warned of two major threats to America in his Farewell Address of January 17, 1961. These stemmed from the emergence of what he called "the military-industrial complex," and from "the technological revolution during recent decades."

As to the first threat, Eisenhower pointed out that "We annually spend on military security more than the net income of all United States corporations," and "have been compelled to create a permanent armaments industry of vast proportions." This industry, in turn, has a "total influence – economic, political, even spiritual – [which] is felt in every city, every State house, every office of the Federal government." As such, he warned that "In the councils of government, we must guard against the acquisition of unwarranted influence, whether sought or unsought, by the military-industrial complex. The potential for the disastrous rise of misplaced power exists and will persist."

The "revolution" in technology posed a second and related threat in Eisenhower's view. Here, "research has become central; it also becomes more formalized, complex, and costly," and "A steadily increasing share is conducted for, by, or at the direction of, the Federal government." This resulted in the creation of "task forces of scientists in laboratories and testing fields," with "a government contract becom[ing] virtually a substitute for intellectual curiosity." The threat thus becomes one of "The prospect of domination of the nation's scholars" by the federal government, and the "danger that public policy could itself become the captive of a scientific-technological elite."

CONCLUSION:

THE INTERSECTING SPHERES OF GOVERNMENT AND BUSINESS

The history of the interrelationship between government and business in the critical 100 year period between 1860 and 1960 illustrates several recurring patterns. Five principal patterns are identifiable. These are: the recurring cycles of regulation and deregulation; the key role played by government-financed infrastructure; the stimulus to business development and expansion effected by war; the importance of governmental protection and funding of technological development; and the role played by the courts in serving as a safety valve to protect businesses from what they saw as overly invasive regulation.

The Recurring Cycles of Regulation and Deregulation

From 1860 to the present, government has oscillated between providing only minimal regulation of business operations and imposing strict and pervasive

169

controls over those operations. In the formative period between 1860 and the dawn of the twentieth century, for example, government stimulated business development through a series of affirmative measures, rather than imposing significant restrictions on business operations. These measures included erecting protective tariffs; funding internal improvements, especially in subsidizing the construction of railroads through land grants, cash outlays, and other subsidies; permitting liberal immigration to provide a skilled workforce and settlers for western lands through homestead laws and other measures; and providing patent protection for a flurry of inventions which promoted the growth of both agriculture and industry.

The favoritism demonstrated toward business by government in the latter half of the nineteenth century led to calls by agricultural interests for stricter regulation of business operations to protect farmers from railroad overcharges, monopoly pricing, and high interest rates. Agricultural organizations including the Grange and several Farmers' Alliances generated political opposition to this laissez-faire approach to business through third political parties such as the Greenbacks and Populists. The agrarian interests were initially successful in securing passage of Granger laws regulating railroads and grain elevators at the state level in the 1870s. Thereafter, their efforts assisted in obtaining federal legislation establishing the Interstate Commerce Commission and enacting antitrust prohibitions against restraints of trade and monopolization. The ambitious efforts of the Populist Party to secure a more pervasive governmental regulation of the economy, including monetary reform and government ownership of key industries, failed, and the Party was marginalized by 1900.

The call for stricter regulation of business continued after 1900 through the efforts of the Progressive Movement. The varied constituencies of this movement combined to effect passage and ratification of the Sixteenth through the Nineteenth Amendments by 1920, providing for a federal income tax, direct election of senators, prohibition, and women's suffrage. In addition, Progressives under Republican presidents Theodore Roosevelt and William Howard Taft obtained the enactment of three separate federal laws regulating railroads and other entities in the Elkins Act, the Hepburn Act, and the Mann-Elkins Act between 1903 and 1910. Moreover, spurred on by muckraking journalists and novelists, Progressives were able to obtain imposition of federal regulation on meat packers and manufacturers of food and drugs in 1906. With the return to power of the Democratic Party from 1913 to 1920, monetary reforms began with the establishment of the Federal Reserve System in 1913, and antitrust enforcement was strengthened through the enactment of the Clayton and Federal Trade Commission Acts in 1914. Agricultural interests were also affected by passage of the Federal Farm Loan and Warehouse Acts of 1916. These legislative victories began an expansion of federal regulation of business which continued and grew through most of the twentieth century. In combination with these new restraints imposed upon business, previous business-friendly policies were discontinued.

In their place came reduction or elimination of protective tariffs and the ending of liberal immigration laws, replaced by harsh restrictions on new immigration from southern and eastern Europe.

With United States entry into World War I, government and business entered a new cycle. Regulation was moderated in favor of a cooperative effort between government and business to address the needs of a militarized economy. Government assisted business in streamlining railroad and other utility operations and standardizing products. When the war ended, and Republicans returned to power in 1921, the regulatory cycle changed again, with a return to the deregulatory policies of the nineteenth century. Tariffs were increased; taxes were lowered; regulatory agencies were shuttered or defunded; and antitrust enforcement was minimized.

The cycle returned to one of heavy regulation as a result of the Great Depression which began in 1929. After the ineffective efforts by President Herbert Hoover to end the depression led to his defeat by Franklin D. Roosevelt in 1932, a series of Democratic "New Deals" imposed wide-ranging restrictions and regulations on business operations. The First New Deal established systems of intensive federal regulation of commercial and investment banking, as well as of agriculture, and initiated direct governmental intervention into the energy and housing sectors of the economy. The Second New Deal expanded regulation even further by securing enhanced rights for labor, enforced by a new federal agency, the National Labor Relations Board. Public utilities were also restricted in their activities, and forced to report to, and obtain approval from, separate federal agencies for some of their activities. A short-lived Third New Deal imposed further regulation on business through the Fair Labor Standards Act, which regulated wages and hours for most sectors of the economy.

With the outbreak of World War II, and American entry into the war in 1941, another cycle began, reverting to the government-business cooperative effort experienced during World War I. From 1941 through 1960, the federal government affirmatively assisted business by funding research and development of new technology, and by granting billions of dollars in defense contracts, leading to the emergence of a new "military-industrial complex." During World War II, antitrust enforcement was minimal, and business profited immensely as a result of massive defense contracts awarded on a cost-plus basis. Because of the scale of production required for the military effort, large businesses were particularly benefited, and their size increased while many smaller businesses failed or were absorbed into their larger competitors. Big business benefitted further at the end of the war when government-financed plant and equipment was sold at fire-sale prices, mainly to large corporations.

The cycles of regulation and deregulation experienced from 1860 to 1960 have continued to the present. Thus, the cycle swung once again to one of heavy federal regulation in the 1960s and 1970s, under both Republican and Democratic presidents. From 1963 to 1980, a flurry of federal regulatory legislation affecting industrial operations was enacted, including several Clean Air Acts, Clean Water Acts, Safe Water

Drinking Acts, and Superfund legislation. In addition, the National Environmental Policy Act established the Environmental Protection Agency to enforce new environmental regulations.

The philosophy of deregulation made a comeback in the 1980s and 1990s with the return of Republican rule, and the deregulation of much of the banking, telecommunications, and airline industries. This legislative and administrative deregulation was complemented by other legislation restricting securities litigation, and by a new antitrust enforcement philosophy based on the teachings of the Chicago School of Economics, which eliminated many so-called "per se" rules of illegality in favor of an enhanced "rule of reason" evaluation of challenged conduct. Under this approach, business was permitted to defend mergers and other practices which had been declared illegal as a matter of law under the prior approach, which emphasized the impact on consumers. In place of this populist focus, the new judicial inquiry asked whether the practice at issue imposed an unreasonable restraint on competition. The preservation of competition - not competitors - became the relevant concern.

Finally, the early years of the twenty-first century witnessed yet another change in the cycle, particularly after the financial crisis which reached its peak in 2007-2009. Massive and detailed regulation to be developed by administrative agencies was mandated by new legislation directed at the banking, financial, and health insurance industries under the Dodd-Frank and Affordable Health Care Acts. In addition, in a return to the approach of the First New Deal, the federal government bailed out failing financial institutions by purchasing stock and warrants under the authority of the Emergency Economic Stabilization Act of 2008. Under the TARP program established by that legislation, the federal government invested almost $250 billion in the securities of more than 200 financial institutions, domestic and foreign, including an investment of $40 billion in the American International Group. Moreover, the government effectively purchased both General Motors and Chrysler, taking massive stock interests in both, and making loans in excess of $18 billion to them.

These instances of increased regulation, some of which began under the Republican Administration of President George W. Bush, reached their apogee during the presidency of Democrat Barack Obama, whose stated goal was to "fundamentally transform America." The efforts of the Obama Administration represent the strictest regulation ever imposed upon business in the United States, creating a massive federal intervention into the economy on a scale never before experienced.

The Importance of Infrastructure

In addition to direct regulation, government also affected business by financing and expanding critical infrastructure. While this has happened throughout American history at the local and state levels, there are three particularly important periods in which government-provided infrastructure was particularly important for the extension of business.

Initially, from the start of the Civil War to the close

of the nineteenth century, Republican Administrations made the building of railroads and the expansion of waterways, harbors, and traditional roadways a top priority. The success of this policy created a national market for goods, and made it possible to link merchants and consumers from the East Coast to the West Coast, and from the North to the South. Without this expansion of infrastructure, interstate commerce would have been lessened and markets kept more localized.

The First and Second New Deals catalyzed a second great expansion of infrastructure through the mechanisms of the Roosevelt Administration's Public Works Administration and Works Progress Administration. These two federal agencies expended some $17 billion and employed millions of unemployed workers. These workers constructed thousands of bridges and highways; erected hundreds of new federal buildings and airports; and developed a wide network of parks.

A third notable expansion of infrastructure funded by the federal government took place as a result of the Interstate Highway Act of 1956. Designed as a defense measure, this legislation also facilitated the development of suburban America, making it possible for builders and construction companies to erect thousands of suburban homes, shopping malls, motels, restaurants, and other amenities, linking suburbia to urban areas by a new highway system of some 41,000 miles.

These three major examples demonstrate how government actions in providing an expansion of infrastructure can have multiple beneficial effects by, among others, supplying new employment opportunities and new markets for businesses. In this context, as Charles Morris has pointed out, it is significant that currently there is a "low level of infrastructure investment relative to GDP."

War As a Business Stimulant

It is an unfortunate truth that war has consistently acted as a stimulant for business, and that government assistance to business has been at its height during wars and other conflicts. We see this pattern as early as the Civil War when railroads expanded to serve the needs of troop transport and supply. World War I, World War II, and the Cold War provide even more graphic examples.

The costs of World War I exceeded $33 billion, and business profited greatly from these governmental expenditures. Manufacturers and farmers profited by increased demand for such items as food, clothing, arms and housing for soldiers. Farmers also profited by supplying new European markets with food when the farmlands of Europe were devastated by land war.

The United States government further assisted American business during World War I by right-sizing railroad operations, eliminating redundancies, and by standardizing manufactured products, greatly reducing variations in size, color, and raw materials.

The costs of World War II were nearly ten times greater than those of World War I, reaching approximately $300 billion. Because of the immediate need for massive amounts of war materials, the federal government was obliged to award billions of dollars of cost-plus contracts to American businesses to supply such items as tanks, ships, planes, military vehicles, arms and munitions for both American troops and those of our allies. In addition, the federal government funded billions of dollars in research and development on new technology which led both to new weapons, including the atomic bomb, rockets, bombers, and missiles, and to new products, including transistors, computers, drugs, and synthetic materials.

As was the case with World War I, government and business worked together in World War II to develop more efficient methods of production which were particularly striking in the manufacture of ships and planes.

In the post-World-War-II era, business was once again a major beneficiary of government spending, initially under the Marshall Plan. Much of the $13 billion funding the Plan supplied was utilized by devastated European countries to rebuild their infrastructure and manufacturing capacity with products produced by American companies.

The huge defense expenditures necessitated by a worldwide war also gave birth to a new "military-industrial complex" which President Eisenhower later identified as a threat to all aspects of American life.

The Cold War continued this expansion of defense industries to meet the perceived threat posed by Russian expansionism and technology, including the launching of the Sputnik satellite in 1957. Indeed, during the 1950s, up to 50% of the federal budget was devoted to defense spending.

Funding and Protecting Technology

One of the key methods by which American government has assisted American business throughout American history was and is the protection of American technology, innovations, and methods of doing business through intellectual property laws, including legal protections afforded patents, copyrights, and trade secrets. While this is been a recurrent pattern from the beginning of the country to the present day, two time periods well illustrate this point.

First, a flurry of new technology and inventions in the last half of the nineteenth century was encouraged and protected by the liberal grant of patents on such innovations as the telephone; the telegraph; railroad engines, motors, brakes and refrigeration cars; and a wide variety of farming implements. Indeed, some 12,000 patents were granted on plows alone during this period.

Second, from the 1940s to recent years, government funding of research and development, in whole or in conjunction with businesses and universities, has led to the invention of hundreds of new products and technologies, particularly in the electronics and pharmaceutical drug industries. These innovations, based upon the findings of such research, have been awarded important legal protections under intellectual property laws, especially in the award of patents, which have conferred industry leadership upon particular companies competing in those industries. One example is the government's development for defense purposes of what we know today as the Internet. That development has spawned a wide-ranging electronics industry which would not have developed in the absence of this governmental breakthrough, which facilitated the founding and expansion of such dominant companies as Apple, Google and Amazon, as well as the invention of cellphones, tablets, and a ubiquity of other electronic products which has affected every American, for good or for ill. To take one other example, Google received funding from the National Science Foundation which assisted it in developing the critical algorithm which fueled the expansion of that company to a position of industry dominance.

A recent troubling note, however, has been sounded in that federal funding for research and development, adjusted for inflation, has experienced a 10% decline since 2009, adversely affecting industries such as defense, energy, pharmaceutical drugs and medicine generally, and agriculture.

Access to the Courts as a Safety Valve for Business

By providing easy access to the courts, government has supplied a critical vehicle to protect businesses from overly invasive regulation. Resort to the courts by business, with the courts oscillating between receptivity to business regulatory challenges and opposition to them, has been another recurrent theme in both the 1860 to 1960 period and thereafter.

From the close of the nineteenth century to 1937, business repeatedly went to court and successfully challenged numerous state and federal laws. Initially, the Supreme Court ruled that business fell within the protections of the Fourteenth Amendment's Due Process and Equal Protection Clauses. The Supreme Court also developed business-friendly legal theories, including freedom of contract and substantive due process, and those theories in turn were employed to invalidate wage and hour, utility rate-making, and railroad rate regulation, as well as a number of other business regulations. This strategy of resort to the courts reached a successful apex with the New Deal cases which struck down the National Industrial Recovery Act and the Agricultural Adjustment Act in 1935 and 1936.

In 1937, the Supreme Court reversed course and began to uphold regulatory legislation enacted in the New Deals and by subsequent administrations. Business was generally unsuccessful thereafter in challenging regulatory laws until the last decades of the twentieth century.

The cycle changed again with the tenures as Chief Justice of William Rehnquist and John Roberts. Business once again won many challenges, limiting, for example, the use of class actions, and the reach of regulatory legislation, including the securities and antitrust laws. This renewed success was far from complete, with the most notable loss coming in the five-to-four decision in *National Federation of Independent Business v. Sebelius* (2012), which upheld the Affordable Health Care Act.

Conclusion: The Triumph of American Industry

In reviewing the history of the relationship and interaction between American business and government in the critical period between 1860 and 1960, it becomes apparent that government can either foster the development and expansion of business or put brakes on it. Of the five patterns explored above, four manifest a consistently affirmative role played by government in promoting American business. First, the creation of a transportation infrastructure in the nineteenth century was an indispensable part of building a national market for the products of American business, as was the building of an interstate highway system for the development of the suburbs in the latter half of the twentieth century. Second, Government spending for defense and under the Marshall Plan, as well as its funding of research and development, promoted the emergence of new markets and new products, including expansion of the electronics and pharmaceutical drug industries. Third, the protections afforded new products, technology, and know-how by intellectual property laws have been a key component fostering the growth of new markets and new businesses. Fourth, access to the judicial branch has provided businesses with a vehicle to challenge, often successfully, legislative efforts to place additional restrictions on business operations.

Business has even profited through many of the cycles of regulation when that regulation outlawed predatory practices which destroyed both competition and competitors, or when regulation created conditions which provided for fair competition. On the other hand, harsh and restrictive regulation can stifle innovation and discourage new investment and the creation of new businesses. Finally, direct government investment in industry, such as happened under the New Deals and under the Obama Administration in the financial and automobile sectors, or government selection of winners and losers by funding some competitors (solar energy, for example) places government in a problematic position vis-a-vis private enterprise, creating a competitor rather than a collaborator. By contrast, cooperation between business and government in such initiatives as the Marshall Plan and multiple private-public research and development projects, has generally proved beneficial to both government and business, as well as to country at large.

One thing remains clear: History demonstrates that government can either assist or stifle business by the actions it chooses to take.

REFERENCES AND SUGGESTED READING

The following general histories of the United States (listed in alphabetical order by author) are especially helpful: Charles and Mary Beard, *The Rise of American Civilization* (MacMillan, 1944); *Alan Brinkley, *The Unfinished Nation: A Concise History of the American People* (3d ed.) (McGraw Hill, 2000); Peter N. Carroll, *We The People: A Brief American History* (Wadsworth Thomson Learning, 2003); *Paul Johnson, *A History of the American People* (HarperCollins, 1998); *Bruce Kuklick, *One Nation Under God: A Political History of the USA* (Palgrave Macmillan, 2009); *Pauline Maier, *Inventing America: A History of the United States* (W.W. Norton, 2003); Samuel Eliot Morison et al, *The Growth of the American Republic* (7th ed.) (Oxford, 1980); Robert V. Remini, *A Short History of the United States* (Harper, 2008). The books marked with an asterisk were assigned as required or recommended texts in various American History courses I have taught at the University of Pennsylvania and Chestnut Hill College.

The following reference books are helpful for supplying dates and general background information:

The Reader's Companion to American History (Eric Foner & John A. Garraty, eds.) (Houghton Mifflin, 1991); *The Oxford Companion to United States History* (Paul S. Boyer, ed.) (Oxford, 2001); Robert A. Rosenbaum, *The Penguin Encyclopedia of American History* (Penguin Reference, 2003); *The Almanac of*

American History (Arthur M. Schlesinger, Jr., gen. ed.) (G.P.Putnam, 1983); Peter Thompson, *Dictionary of American History: From 1763 To The Present* (Checkmark Books, 2000).

CHAPTER 1: THE CIVIL WAR: CRUSHING THE SLAVE POWER

Chapter One is based on my 2002 paper, "Half Slave and Half Free: The Long Road to the Civil War," which I have substantially updated based on recent scholarship. For an overview of that scholarship, see Michael E. Woods, "What Twenty-First-Century Historians Have Said about the Causes of Disunion: A Civil War Sesquicentennial Review of the Recent Literature," *The Journal of American History*, Vol.99, No.2 (September 2012), at 415-439.

For the most recent, census-based count of the Civil War dead, see J. David Hacker, "A Census-Based Count of the Civil War Dead," *Civil War History*, Vol. LVII, No. 4 (2011), at 307-348.

For an explanation of proximate cause and substantial contributing factors in determining legal causation, see American Law Institute, *Restatement (Second) of Torts*, sections 431-433.

On the social and economic differences between North and South and the course of industrialization, see James M. McPherson's books: *Battle Cry of Freedom: The Civil War Era* (Oxford, 1988); *Drawn with the Sword* (Oxford, 1996); and *Abraham Lincoln and the Second American Revolution* (Oxford, 1991), and also:

Marc Egnal, *Clash of Extremes: The Economic Origins of the Civil War* (Hill and Wang, 2009); William W. Freehling, *The Reintegration of American History: Slavery and the Civil War* (Oxford, 1994); Michael F. Holt, *The Fate of Their Country: Politicians, Slavery Extension, and the Coming of the Civil War* (Hill and Wang, 2004); Daniel Walker Howe, *What Hath God Wrought: The Transformation of America, 1815-1848* (Oxford, 2007); Walter Licht, *Industrializing America: The Nineteenth Century* (Johns Hopkins University Press, 1995); David Donald, *Charles Sumner and the Coming of the Civil War* (Knopf, 1967), at 289-311; and Forrest McDonald, *States' Rights and the Union: Imperium in Imperio, 1776-1876* (University Press of Kansas, 2000), at 104-110.

On differences in the Northern and Southern legal systems, see Edward F. Mannino, *Shaping America: The Supreme Court and American Society* (University of South Carolina Press, 2009), at 38-43; Kermit L. Hall, *The Magic Mirror* (Oxford, 1989), at 119-126, 134-136; Kermit L. Hall, William M. Wiecek, and Paul Finkelman, *American Legal History: Cases and Materials* (2d ed.) (Oxford, 1996), at 171-186.

On the demise of the Whig Party, see James M. McPherson, *Battle Cry of Freedom*, Chapter 4.

J.G. Randall's article on "The Blundering Generation" appeared in the *Mississippi Valley Historical Review* (June 1940), at 27.

The Supreme Court decisions on slavery and the Fugitive Slave Act are discussed in detail in Mannino, *Shaping America,* at 31-37. Different portions of the correspondence between President Buchanan and Justices Catron and Greer relating to the anticipated decision in the *Dred Scott* case may be found in Kenneth M. Stamp, *America in 1857: A Nation on the Brink* (Oxford, 1990), at 90-92; Peter Irons, *A People's History of the Supreme Court* (rev. ed.) (Penguin Books, 2006), at 170-171; and *Great Cases in Constitutional Law* (Robert P. George, ed.) (Princeton University Press, 2000), at 73.

For a detailed argument that the Civil War did not initiate nineteenth-century industrial development, see Walter Licht, *Industrializing America*, at 79-101

CHAPTER 2: THE GREAT PUSH TO ECONOMIC DEVELOPMENT

For the economic development of the United States in the nineteenth century after the Civil War, see Glenn Porter, *The Rise of Big Business 1860-1920* (3d ed.) (Harlan Davidson, 2006); Charles R. Morris, *The Dawn of Innovation: The First American Industrial Revolution* (Public Affairs, 2012), at 233-589; Walter Licht, *Industrializing America*, at 102-132; Alexander Keyssar, *Inventing America*, at 563-593; II Morison et al., *The Growth of the American Republic*, at 3-147.

On California, see Alexander Saxton, *The Indispensable Enemy: Labor and the Anti-Chinese Movement in California* (University of California, 1971, 1995).

For the development of the tobacco industry, see Robert F. Durden, *Bold Entrepreneur: A Life of James B. Duke* (Carolina Academic Press, 2003).

CHAPTER 3: THE ADVENT OF REGULATION: THE PRODUCERS STRIKE BACK

For histories of the Farmers' Alliances and the Populists, see Lawrence Goodwyn, *The Populist Moment: A Short History of the Agrarian Revolt in America* (Oxford, 1978); John D. Hicks, *The Populist Revolt: A History of the Farmers' Alliance and the People's Party* (University of Nebraska, 1961); Michael Kazin, *The Populist Persuasion: An American History* (rev. ed.) (Cornell, 1995), at 27-46; Robert C. McMath, Jr., *American Populism: A Social History, 1877-1898* (Hill & Wang, 1992); Norman Pollack, *The Populist Response to Industrial America: Midwestern Populist Thought* (Harvard, 1962); Charles Postel, *The Populist Vision* (Oxford, 2007); Richard Stiller, *Queen of Populists: The Story of Mary Elizabeth Lease* (Thomas Y. Crowell Co., 1970).

The following two Readers contain many selections from Populist writers: *The Populist Mind* (Norman Pollack ed.) (Bobbs-Merrill Co., 1967); *A Populist Reader* (George B. Tindall, ed.) (Harper Torchbooks, 1966).

For the quotation regarding control of the Pennsylvania legislature by the Rockefeller interests, see "Robber barons and silicon sultans," *The Economist*, January 3, 2015.

The Supreme Court cases mentioned in the text are discussed and analyzed in Mannino, *Shaping America*, at 75-84.

On the Election of 1896 and the campaign strategies

of McKinley and Bryan, see the books cited above and Kevin Phillips, *William McKinley* (Times Books, 2003), at 66-84, and Michael Kazin, *A Godly Hero: The Life of William Jennings Bryan* (Alfred A. Knopf, 2006), at 45-79.

CHAPTER 4: THE SECOND ROUND OF REGULATION: THE PROGRESSIVE MOVEMENT

For a detailed history of the Progressive Movement, see Michael McGerr, *A Fierce Discontent: The Rise and Fall of the Progressive Movement in America, 1870-1920* (Free Press, 2003). See also Doris Kearns Goodwin, *The Bully Pulpit: Theodore Roosevelt, William Howard Taft, and the Golden Age of Journalism* (Simon & Schuster, 2013), which is particularly good on the history of *McClure's Magazine* and the journalism of the muckraking period generally; Jackson Lears, *Rebirth of A Nation: The Making of Modern America, 1877-1920* (Harper, 2009), Chapters 5-7 and Conclusion; James A. Morone, *Hellfire Nation: The Politics of Sin in American History* (Yale University Press, 2003), Chapters 9-11; Eric Rauchway, *Murdering McKinley: The Making of Theodore Roosevelt's America* (Hill & Wang, 2003).

The Progressive Movement in the Western states is covered in Richard White, *"It's Your Misfortune and None of My Own": A New History of the American West* (University of Oklahoma Press, 1991), at 378-384. For a discussion of *Pierce v. Society of Sisters*, see Mannino, *Shaping America*, at 146-147.

For the professionalization of higher education,

see Bruce Kuklick, *The Rise of American Philosophy: Cambridge, Massachusetts, 1860-1930* (Yale University Press, 1977).

For the evolution of American business, see Glenn Porter, *The Rise of Big Business: 1860-1920*, Chapter 3; Jonathan Levy, *Freaks of Fortune: The Emerging World of Capitalism and Risk in America* (Harvard University Press, 2012), especially Chapter 8, "The Trust Question."

For Theodore Roosevelt's presidency, see Theodore Roosevelt, *An Autobiography* (Charles Scribner's Sons, 1920), especially Chapters X , XII, and XIII; Edmund Morris, *Theodore Rex* (Random House, 2001). See also Louis Auchincloss, *Theodore Roosevelt* (Times Books, 2001); Michael Beschloss, *Presidential Courage: Brave Leaders and How They Changed America, 1789-1989* (Simon & Schuster, 2007), Chapters 17-20.

For an analysis of the *Northern Securities* case and the Supreme Court's antitrust decisions of the period, see Mannino, *Shaping America*, at 93-100.

On the Panic of 1907, see Ron Chernow, *The House of Morgan: An American Banking Dynasty and the Rise of Modern Finance* (Atlantic Monthly Press, 1990), at 121-128; Goodwin, *The Bully* Pulpit, at 527-530; and Levy, *Freaks of Fortune*, at 268-272.

For the Election of 1912, see James Chace, *1912: Wilson, Roosevelt, Taft & Debs – The ElectionThat Changed the Country* (Simon & Schuster, 2004); Edmund Morris, *Colonel Roosevelt* (Random House, 2010), Chapters 5-12; Doris Goodwin, *The Bully Pulpit*, Chapters 25-29.

On Wilson's presidency, see H.W. Brands, *Woodrow Wilson* (Times Books, 2003). For negative appraisals criticizing Wilson for starting the era of big government on the national level, see Paul D. Moreno, *The American State From the Civil War to the New Deal: The Twilight of Constitutionalism and the Triumph of Progressivism* (Cambridge University Press, 2013), Chapters 11-13; Andrew P. Napolitano, *Theodore and Woodrow: How Two American Presidents Destroyed Constitutional Freedoms* (Thomas Nelson, 2012). For a positive view of Wilson's presidency, see II Morison et al., *The Growth of the American Republic*, Chapter XIV.

CHAPTER 5: FROM CONFRONTATION TO COOPERATION: WORLD WAR I, BUSINESS, AND THE RETURN OF REPUBLICAN RULE

For an analysis of the impact of World War I on business and government, see David M. Kennedy, *Over Here: The First World War and American Society* (25th Anniversary Edition) (Oxford University Press, 2004), especially Chapter 2.

For discussions of the Republican policies of the 1920s, see David Cannadine, *Mellon: An American Life* (Albert A. Knopf, 2006), especially Chapters 9-13; Amity Shlaes, *Coolidge* (HarperCollins, 2013), especially Chapters 7-15; David Greenberg, *Calvin Coolidge* (Times Books, 2006); William E. Leuchtenburg, *Herbert Hoover* (Times Books, 2009); David M. Kennedy, *Freedom From Fear: The American People in Depression and War, 1929-1945* (Oxford University Press, 1999), Chapters 1-3; and Arthur M. Schlesinger,

Jr., *The Crisis of the Old Order 1919-1933* (Houghton Mifflin Company, 1957).

For the Supreme Court's decisions on wage and hour and other business issues discussed in the text, see Mannino, *Shaping America*, at 84-93. On the *Lochner* case, see id. at 86-88, and David E. Bernstein, *Rehabilitating Lochner: Defending Individual Rights against Progressive Reform* (University of Chicago Press, 2011).

CHAPTER 6: REGULATION WITH A VENGEANCE: FDR'S NEW DEALS

For discussions of the three New Deals and the varying approaches to economic regulation taken in New Deal legislation, see Jonathan Alter, *The Defining Moment: FDR's Hundred Days and the Triumph of Hope* (Simon & Schuster, 2006), at 207-337; Conrad Black, *Franklin Delano Roosevelt: Champion of Freedom* (Public Affairs, 2003), Chapters 6-10; Alan Brinkley, *Franklin Delano Roosevelt* (Oxford University Press, 2010); Roy Jenkins, *Franklin Delano Roosevelt* (Times Books, 2003), Chapters 4-5; David M. Kennedy, *Freedom From Fear*, Chapters 4-12; Paul D. Moreno, *The American State from the Civil War to the New Deal*, Chapters 18-23; Arthur M. Schlesinger, Jr., *The Coming of the New Deal* (Houghton Mifflin Co.,1959) and *The Politics of Upheaval* (Houghton Mifflin Co.,1960); and Amity Shlaes, *The Forgotten Man: A New History of the Great Depression* (HarperCollins 2007), Chapters 5-9, 11-13.

For the investment community's reaction to the New

Deals, see Chernow, *The House of Morgan*, Chapters 18-19.

For the Supreme Court's decisions on the NIRA, the AAA, and other New Deal legislation, as well as the Court-Packing Plan, see Mannino, *Shaping America*, Chapter 6.

The calculations of Professors Cole and Ohanian, and the quotation from Professor Ohanian, appear and are discussed in Meg Sullivan, "FDR's policies prolonged Depression by 7 years, UCLA economists calculate," UCLA Newsroom, August 10, 2004.

CHAPTER 7: THE MILITARY-INDUSTRIAL COMPLEX: WORLD WAR II, THE COLD WAR, AND AMERICAN BUSINESS

On World War II, I have relied heavily upon Chapter 18, "The War of Machines," of David M. Kennedy's *Freedom From Fear* for the statistics recounted in this chapter. For further data and other information on World War II and business, see Andrew Roberts, *The Storm of War: A New History of the Second World War* (Harper, 2011), at 89, 176, 194-199, and 214-215, and Thomas K. McCraw, *American Business Since 1920: How It Worked* (2d ed.) (Harlan Davidson, Inc., 2009), Chapter 3.

James T. Patterson's *Grand Expectations: The United States, 1945-1974* (Oxford University Press, 1996) was helpful on many of the post-World-War-II statistics set forth in this chapter. Additional material on the period is found in Thomas K. McCraw, *American Business Since 1920*, Chapters 4, 5, and 8.

On the Marshall Plan, see Charles L. Mee, Jr., *The Marshall Plan* (Touchtone, Simon & Schuster, 1984).

On IBM and the computer industry, see McCraw, Chapter 8, and H.W. Brands, *Masters of Enterprise: Giants of American Business from John Jacob Astor and J.P. Morgan to Bill Gates and Oprah Winfrey* (Free Press, 1999), Chapter 10. For the beginnings and subsequent history of McDonald's, see McCraw, Chapter 5, and Brands, Chapter 16.

For an exploration of the thought of George Kennan and a growing group of defense intellectuals, see Bruce Kuklick, *Blind Oracles: Intellectuals and War from Kennan to Kissinger* (Princeton University Press, 2006).

CONCLUSION: THE INTERSECTING
SPHERES OF GOVERNMENT AND BUSINESS

For business and economic developments after 1960, see generally McCraw, Chapters 4-8; James T. Patterson, *Restless Giant: The United States from Watergate to Bush v. Gore* (Oxford University Press, 2005); and Charles R. Morris, *Comeback: America's New Economic Boom* (PublicAffairs, 2013).

For a discussion and analysis of the post-Civil-War decisions of the Supreme Court affecting business, see Mannino, *Shaping America*, Chapters 5, 6, and 9. On the recent, and mainly business-friendly, decisions of the Roberts Court, see also Edward F. Mannino, "The Roberts Court and Business: Twelve Key Decisions," at www.edmannino.com/blog, posted on July 2, 2013.

INDEX

A

Abelman v. Booth (1859) 33
Adkins v. Children's Hospital (1923) 122,144
Administrative State 150-151
Agricultural Adjustment Acts (1933, 1938)
    129,133-135,149-150
Agricultural Marketing Act (1929) 124
"American System" (Henry Clay) 41,42
Antitrust Laws 91-97,99-100,108-110,114,150

B

Bank failures 126,132-133
Banking Act (1935) 146
Bank of Augusta v. Earle (1839) 21
Barker, Wharton 81
Big Business
    94-96,104,109,119-120,135-136,154-155,164-168
Briscoe v. Bank of Kentucky (1837) 26
Brown, John 18
Brandeis, Louis 104
Bryan, William Jennings 4,76,78-79
Buck v. Bell (1927) 88
Buchanan, James 32,36
Bunting v. Oregon (1917) 121

C

Calhoun, John C. 15-16
Charles River Bridge v. Warren Bridge (1837) 20-21
Chicago, Milwaukee & St. Paul Ry. Co. v. Minnesota (1890) 74-75
Clayton Act (1914) 109,120
Cold War 7-8,165-166,178
Coolidge, Calvin 117,119,122-123
Coughlin, Charles 140-141,146
County of Santa Clara v. Southern Pacific RR Co. (1886) 74
Courts 20-24,72-76,95-96,120-122,180-181

D

Debs, In Re (1895) 76
Defense Industry 153-154,156,164-168

E

Eisenhower, Dwight 8,166-168
Election of 1912 102-105
Elkins Act (1903) 92-93
Emergency Banking Act (1933) 132
Emergency Relief Act (1935) 142
Eugenics 87-88

F

Fair Labor Standards Act (1938) 7,149
Farm Economy 53,56-57,61-62,110-111,113,120,124
Farmers' Alliances 4,55,58,60,72,81
Federal Farm Board 124

Federal Farm Loan Act (1916) 110
Federal Home Loan Bank 127
Federal Reserve Act (1913) 5,108
Food Administration 115-116
Fuel Administration 115
Fugitive Slave Law (1850) 29-30

G
Glass-Steagall Act (1933) 132,146
Gold Standard Act (1934) 133
Grange/Patrons of Husbandry 4,58,72
Granger Cases (1877) 73-74
Great Depression 125,136,155

H
Harding, Warren 116-117,118,120,121-122
Hepburn Act (1906) 93
Homestead Acts 36,48-49
Hoover, Herbert 6,115,118,122-127

I
Immigration 44-45,50,89
Income Tax 72,107,116,119,125,142-143
Industry 39-47,53-54
    in South 46-47
    in West 53-54
Infrastructure
    27,41-44,115,137,138-139,142,162,175-177
Interstate Commerce Commission 63,93
Interstate Highway Act (1956) 162

J

Jefferson, Thomas 14-15

K

Kansas-Nebraska Act (1854) 18-19,30
Kennan, George 165
Kennedy, John 166
Knight Co. v. United States (1895) 76-77

L

Labor issues 44-45,58-59,60-61,92,121-122,162-163
Lease, Mary 55-56,58,70
Lincoln, Abraham 12,19,30,42
Lochner v. New York (1905) 121
Long, Huey 140

M

Mann-Elkins Act (1910) 101
Marshall Plan 163-164,178,182
McClure, S.S./McClures's Magazine 83-84
McKinley, William 4,76,79,91-92
Meat Inspection Act (1906) 93
Mellon, Andrew 119,131
Military-Industrial Complex 166-167
Morrill Land Grant Act (1862) 37
Morrill Tariff Act (1861) 36
Morgan, J.P. 95-98,120,131
Muller v. Oregon (1908) 121
Munn v. Illinois (1877) 73,75,103

N

National Bank Act (1863) 37

National Credit Corporation 126

National Housing Act (1934) 139

National Industrial Recovery Act/NRA (1933)
    135-137

National Labor Relations Act (1935) 143-144

NLRB v. Jones & Laughlin Steel Corp. (1937) 144,148

Native Americans 50-51,52

Northern Securities Co. v. United States (1904)
    95-96,129

P

Pacific Railway Act (1862) 36-37

Panic of 1907 96-98,108

Pollock v. Farmers Loan & Trust Co. (1895) 76

Populist Party 3-4,65-81

Populist Party Platform 4,66-72,105

Progressive Movement 4,81-111

Progressive Party 102-103,117-118

Prohibition 85-86,89-90

Public Utilities Holding Company Act (1935) 7,145

Public Works Administration 137

Pure Food & Drug Act (1906) 93

R

Railroads 41-44,48,57,59,63-64,101,115

Reconstruction Finance Corporation 127,132,154

Regulation, Cycles of
    63-65,92-93,101,108-111,128-151,169-175

R&D spending 160-161

Roosevelt, Franklin 6,117,128-151,152-154
Roosevelt, Theodore 5,82-84,91-99,102-106
"Roosevelt Recession" 147,149

S

Schechter Poultry Corp. v. United States (1935) 136-137,151
Scott v. Sandford (1857) 28,31,33
Securities Act (1933) 136
Securities Exchange Act (1934) 136-137
Segregation 88-89
Sherman Antitrust Act (1890) 64-65,76-77
Smyth v. Ames (1898) 75-76
Social Gospel Movement 4,86
Social Security Act (1935) 6,141-142
Supreme Court of the United States 20-22,73-76,95-96,120-122,136-137,144-148,149-150,180-181
Swift v. Tyson (1842) 21-22

T

Taft, William Howard 5,98-102,105-106,121-122
Taft-Hartley Act (1947) 162
Tariffs 15-16,25,40-41,57,62,100-101,107-108,116,118-119
Technology 45-46,52-53,157-161,167-168,179-180
Tennessee Valley Authority 138-139
Trade Associations 85

U

United States v. Butler (1936) 134-135
United States v. Hanway (1851) 30

W

Wabash, St. Louis & Pacific Ry. Co. v. Illinois (1886) 74

War Industries Board 113-114

War Production Board 154

Warehouse Act (1916) 69,110-111

West Coast Hotel v. Parrish (1937) 144,148

Wickard v. Filburn (1942) 129, 144-145

Wilson, Woodrow 5,36,89,102,104-111,112-116

Works Progress Administration 6,142

World War I 5,112-116,123,177

World War II 7,152-159,177-178

ABOUT THE AUTHOR

Edward F. Mannino is a lawyer and historian. He is an high honors graduate of the University of Pennsylvania and its Law School, and has taught law courses at Temple University Law School, and history courses and seminars at the University of Pennsylvania and Chestnut Hill College. The subjects he has taught include The United States From the Civil War to the Twenty-First Century, U.S. Legal History, The Supreme Court in American History, The American Catholic Experience, Environmental Law, and Trial Practice.

He is the author of five books on law and history, including *Shaping America: The Supreme Court and American Society* (University of South Carolina Press, 2009) and *Faith of Our Fathers: An American Catholic History* (WingSpan Press, 2012).

Mannino has been named as one of the "Nations Top Litigators," and also as one of the top ten trial lawyers in Pennsylvania by the *National Law Journal.* Chambers USA's publication, *America's Leading Lawyers for Business,* noted that he was a "well-prepared, thorough and aggressive litigator," "extremely sharp," and had a "razor-sharp mind."

Mannino is a member of the Organization of American Historians, the Fellowship of Catholic Scholars, the Order of Malta, and the Pennsylvania Society. He also has served as an Overseer of the Faculty of Arts and Sciences of the University of Pennsylvania and as a Commonwealth Trustee of Temple University. He was appointed to the latter position by Governor Robert P. Casey of Pennsylvania.

Mannino lives in Gwynedd Valley, Pennsylvania, with his wife, Toni O'Connell. He blogs on the Supreme Court and on American law, history, and culture at www.edmannino.com/blog and tweets at @Edmannino.

Lightning Source UK Ltd.
Milton Keynes UK
UKHW010700271020
372315UK00002B/327

9 781595 945907